Is There Any Meat on the Bones? What a descriptive title for the contents! The collection of scriptures, experiences, examples capture areas in all of our lives. Dr. Sandra's insight and expertise of God's Word is exhibited in application to the Christian life. We clearly see God's pathway for self-examination, and experience His love, forgiveness, and joy through the freedom he has for us. This book is also a teaching manual for leadership and laypersons to help others come into the fullness of God's plan. Dr. Sandra's years of prayer, study, ministry, and herself having victory during the "hard times" has produced this beautiful portrait of the love of God. Thank you for writing this much needed book.

Dr. Gwen Aldridge
Lamesa Christian Fellowship
Lamesa, Texas

In this must-read book, *Is There Any Meat on the Bones?* Dr. Sandra Gay has provided an in-depth look at pitfalls the enemy of our soul would desire us to focus on—the hurts of life. With her revelation from God's perspective concerning the lives of His children, it remains clear that what satan meant for evil, God will turn for our good! We have used the nuggets found throughout this on-time message, and are seeing results in the lives of the hearers. Every minister of the Gospel will glean much wisdom from these pages to deliver to those whom God has entrusted them with, bringing these people healing truths and freedom.

Pastors Victor and Malieka Hall,
Mountain Faith Ministry
Knoxville, Tennessee

I met Dr. Sandra Gay through another ministry relationship, and she has impacted my life in an extraordinary way through her wisdom, knowledge, and poise. When I was told of her authoring a book, I knew it would be filled with a wealth of life's experiences.

Upon reviewing *Is There Any Meat on the Bones?* I endorse the truths from the Word of God that Dr. Sandra Gay has brought forth to help readers move from the physical and emotional trauma that occurred through their lives into new life with Jesus Christ. This book is a powerful tool, which, if used correctly, will enable those seeking restoration from past experiences to find it by giving them a step-by-step process to total freedom. Each chapter exposes those things that are associated with what has caused the imprisonment of the mind, will and emotions—the soul—of individuals.

The informational approach that Dr. Gay uses is phenomenal, and it brings awareness to the healing power of Jesus Christ, which is given to those who accept Him as Lord and Savior. This book brings clarity to the factors that blinds the minds of people and causes them not to live in total freedom.

Bishop Henry Frank Eluett,
Founder and Pastor, The River Church
Margate, Florida

Reading Dr. Sandra Gay's insightful book is like taking a graduate level course in the ministries of Inner Healing and Deliverance. Her fine-tuned skill of "rightly dividing the word of truth," combined with practical application and experience, truly make Dr. Gay a herald in God's Kingdom. *Is There Any Meat on the Bones?* gives you greater understanding and revelation, while providing a roadmap for the spiritual and emotional healing you've been seeking!

Drs. Simon and Trish Presland
Senior Associate Pastors, Evangel Christian Church
Deans, Christian Counseling Institute
Overseers, Spiritual Warfare Ministries
Roseville, Michigan

Is There Any *Meat* on the *Bones?*

Is There Any *Meat* on the *Bones?*

Looking **Beyond** Your Hurts **To** Receive Emotional Healing

Dr. Sandra R. Gay

Is There Any Meat on the Bones?
Copyright © 2023 Dr. Sandra R. Gay

Softcover ISBN: 978-1-950880-08-9
eBook ISBN: 978-1-950880-09-6

All rights reserved. No part of this publication may be reproduced, distributed, or transmitted in any form or by any means, including photocopying, recording, or other electronic or mechanical methods, without the prior written permission of the publisher, except in the case of brief quotations embodied in critical reviews and certain other noncommercial uses permitted by copyright law. For permission requests, write to the publisher, addressed "Attention: Permissions Coordinator," at the address below.

Unless otherwise stated, all Scripture is taken from the New King James Version®. Copyright © 1982 by Thomas Nelson. Used by permission. All rights reserved.

Scripture quotations from The Authorized (King James) Version. Rights in the Authorized Version in the United Kingdom are vested in the Crown. Reproduced by permission of the Crown's patentee, Cambridge University Press.

Holy Bible, New Living Translation, copyright © 1996, 2004, 2015 by Tyndale House Foundation. Used by permission of Tyndale House Publishers, Inc., Carol Stream, Illinois 60188. All rights reserved.

Scripture quotations taken from the Amplified® Bible (AMPC), Copyright © 1954, 1958, 1962, 1964, 1965, 1987 by The Lockman Foundation. Used by permission. www.lockman.org

Table of Contents

Acknowlegements xi
Foreword xv
Introduction xix
#You Too? xxv

Part 1 **Why Were You Apprehended?** 1
Chapter 1: God's Perspective 7
Chapter 2: God's Purpose 15
Chapter 3: God's Plan 25

Part 2 **Is it a Family Affair?** 35
Chapter 4: Parents and Others in Authority 45
Chapter 5: In The House But Not in the Family 53
Chapter 6: Curses 63

Part 3   **Is It Really About You?**. 75

Chapter 7: Make No Bones About It! 85

Chapter 8: Error of Entitlement 91

Chapter 9: The Pit of Pride. 101

Part 4   **How Is The Meat Separated?**. 111

Chapter 10: God's Surgical Scalpel. 125

Chapter 11: The Communion Table 133

Part 5   **Children, Have You Any Meat?** 139

Chapter 12: What Are Protein Blockers? 147

Chapter 13: What the Enemy Meant for Evil 155

Chapter 14: Could the Enemy Have Any Fears Concerning You? 163

Chapter 15: A Message to Leaders 171

Epilogue. 181

Suggested Reading List. 187

About the Author. 189

Acknowlegements

All glory, honor, and praise to the God of Abraham, Isaac, and Israel for placing it upon my heart to write this book and for guiding me every step of the way. You are such an awesome wonder, who wouldn't serve a God like you!

To my husband, Apostle Alonzo T. Gay, Sr. for being the one God chose to bring completion in my life. You have truly been my best friend, Priest, Prophet, and Pastor. Thank you for who God made you to be and for the love you have towards Him and His people. It is a blessing to be married to you and to co-labor with you in the gospel.

To my children, Marvin, Stephen, Pamela, and Jennifer, my four special gifts from God. I am so proud of you and how you have exceeded me in so many ways. What a blessing it is to be chosen by God to be your mother.

Rev. Willie W. Clemmons and his wife, Alice, for leading me to my precious savior Jesus Christ forty-seven years ago at Bethel A.M.E. Church in Adrian, Michigan. Thank you for being godparents to my children and embracing our family for many years. You always spoke to my potential when I couldn't see it in myself. Thank you for your prayers and patience towards me while Christ was being formed in me.

To Mother Elizabeth (Estelle) McLemore who adopted me as her spiritual daughter and taught me so many things about being a woman, wife, and mother that I missed growing up without my biological mother.

Dr. Sherill Piscopo of Evangel Christian Churches in Roseville, Michigan, who continues to be an excellent role model of women in ministry. Thank you for allowing God to use you to develop the teaching gift within me and for mentoring me in Inner Healing, intercessory prayer, and the ministry of dance. When I grow up, I'm going to be just like you!

To my Acts Ministries family of Eagle Lake, Florida, for the love, encouragement, and prayer support given me as I took on this assignment. Many thanks to our Apostolic Inner Healing and Deliverance Team for laying down their lives to bring healing and restoration to so many.

To two of my faithful leaders, Rev. Sharon Thompson and Rev. Rosemary Hinos, who co-labored with me at the Southwest Detroit Outreach Church of Evangel. Thank you for the opportunity we had to grow together.

To my editor, Simon Presland, for his patience, encouragement, and kindness towards me along the way as I traveled the uncharted territory of authorship.

Special dedication to, and in loving memory of Dr. Gennaro (Jerry) Piscopo, (1951-2021), whom we all called Bishop. He relocated to his heavenly home before this book was completed. A true Apostle and a man of faith who panted after the heart of God. This book reflects the love, patience, encouragement, and impartation I received from him over the years as my mentor, training and equipping me in ministry leadership and deliverance. Bishop taught me how to recognize the voice of God, to have intimacy with Christ, to operate in the gifts of Holy Spirit, and the benefits of maintaining a prayer journal. He will always have a special place in my heart because he loved and accepted me in my brokenness and allowed God to use him as one of His instruments to promote healing in me. I am one of many thousands of lives Bishop's ministry has touched during his time on the earth. He is missed tremendously but his legacy lives on in me and so many others. You are gone but will never be forgotten!

Foreword

Of all the many books I have studied and adapted concepts from to my own repertoire and experiences, this book, *Is There Any Meat on the Bones?* by Dr. Sandra Gay surpasses them all!

I have had the honor of knowing this woman of God for over thirty-six years, as a spiritual daughter, pastor, prophetess, mom, and wife. Dr. Sandra is a discerner, a "quiet giant," a lover of God, and people. She has gained much experience and knowledge in her lifetime by "eating the meat and gently spitting out the bones."

Dr. Sandra's natural ability as a teacher shines, and in this book she drives home several points that the reader must meditate on, in order to see the finished purposes of God. She causes us to examine our lives from womb to eventual tomb, while surrendering to God our all in the best way we know how to. For instance, I have never pondered the fact that God "apprehended" me, but Dr. Sandra points this out. Often, we think *we* choose God. In reality, He chose each one of us. He snatches us out of the grip of the enemy, and sets us in a place where we must choose whom we will serve, and then takes us through a process. It is this "process" that illuminates why this book must be applied to our lives. We are "remade" layer by layer when He is truly Lord over our lives, and this is a daily process we must undergo. As Jeremiah 18:4 says, "but the vessel he was making of clay was spoiled in the hand of the potter; so he remade it in to another vessel, as it pleased the potter to make...."

There is a realization that comes to us through the pages of this book: Our purpose for life is about pleasing God, and to bring comfort to others through the ministry of inner healing and deliverance. This is a revelation to many because, so often, we think we exist to live, work, and enjoy life, with a visit to God's house once a week. Not so. It's all about Jesus and seeing life from His viewpoint, walking in His peace, focusing on His promises. This is a habitation not a visitation!

This book is for every person who desires to see God's plan come to fruition in their lives. Dr. Sandra enforces the need to seek God like never before. It is in that place, where we surrender our plans to God, that he can have His way. Of course, we find it is much better than our original plan! As Proverbs 19:21 tells us, "Many plans are in a man's mind, but it is the Lord's purpose for him, that will stand (be carried out)."

Dr. Sandra instructs us to look for God in every circumstance of our lives. Many of us think that He "'goes on vacation" or is "out to lunch" when the trials of life come our way. We think we can handle a particular circumstance, but God says, "I want to be involved in every decision, happening, or event in your life!"

Dr. Sandra also notes that the purpose of this writing is to focus on God and move beyond the hurts of life, and see Him for who He truly is—our loving Heavenly Father—and what He purposes for our lives. We are moved to do this through seeking Him, reading His Word, and walking with the Holy Spirit. Our main assignment is to be the "church" and win the lost.

This book is a message for every generation ... all meat no bones!

I Corinthians 10:11 tells us, "Now these things happened to them as an example and warning ... they were written as instruction whom the ends of the ages have come."

Eat well and live!

Dr. Sherill Piscopo
Senior Pastor, Evangel Christian Churches
Overseer, EACM, Evangel Association of
Churches & Ministries
Author: *Spiritual Warfare: A Comprehensive Guide
to Personal Healing and Deliverance*

Introduction

There is a popular saying I have heard most of my life, as I'm sure many of you have: Eat the meat and spit out the bones. This saying was used frequently by our late Bishop, Dr. Jerry Piscopo, as we elders were being groomed for leadership. It was a tool to help us avoid murmuring and complaining, or developing a critical and judgmental spirit when we encountered controversy. We learned how to trust God to do the separating and to focus on that which was relevant to God's Kingdom purpose, instead of that which was counterproductive.

This saying resonated in my spirit for this book to bring encouragement to members in the Body of Christ who feel they have become a victim of what some label as "church hurt." I also want to bring understanding and help for those who desire to be released from a cycle of woundedness affecting their spiritual, emotional, mental, and physical growth in Christ.

The following are some of the topics of discovery you will find in this book:

- What is the meat?
- What might be keeping us from seeing the meat?
- How to separate the meat from the bones?
- How to recognize what's really bone(s) and what's a tool God will use for our processing.

What we focus on is what will occupy our mind, will, and emotions, and what we will advance towards.

This book is mainly about focus. What we focus on is what will occupy our mind, will, and emotions, and what we will advance towards.

The word *purpose* is defined as: The reason why something is done or used. The aim or intention of something: the feeling of being determined to do or achieve something; the aim or goal of a person; what a person is trying to do, become, etc.[1] For Christians to walk in purpose, there are two important questions that must be answered to keep us on course: why were we born and why were we born again?

As followers of Christ, we have been commissioned to follow His example in fulfilling His purpose for coming to earth. *1 John 3:8b states: "…For this purpose the Son of God was manifested, that he might destroy the works of the devil."* How do you destroy the works of the devil? By doing what he doesn't want you to do—get realigned with your purpose and separating yourself from those unrelated things causing you to detour from it.

---

[1] https:/www.Merriam-webster.com

Introduction

Whether layperson or leader, I pray that you will read something that will awaken within you the awareness of some strategies the enemy of our soul uses to hinder you from walking in the plan and purposes of God. The Apostle Paul gives us an excellent reason to be aware of Satan's strategies; *"Lest Satan should take advantage of us; for we are not ignorant of his devices" (2 Corinthians 2:11).*

The title of this book and each section is introduced as a question for contemplation. As we journey to seek answers to these questions—from the examples recorded in God's word, my personal experience, and the examples of others—I believe the following will occur:

1. Your attention will be captured.
2. You will focus on discovering answers to the questions.
3. Your focused attention will pave the way for the impartation of revelation.
4. The revelation imparted will pave the way for application, restoration, activation and transformation.

Selah Moment: This book was not written to just be read through; there will be opportunity in each section to pause and reflect with a desire to gain God's truth on the particular subject matter presented. These opportunities to pause and reflect I call "Selah Moments." *Selah* is a Hebrew word that is used seventy-one times in the book of Psalms and three times in Habakkuk. There are many interpretations of the word Selah. For the purpose of this book, I chose the particular application of this word expressed in the following article: [2]

One possible Hebrew word related to Selah, is calah, which mean "to hang" or "to measure or weigh in the balances." Referring to wisdom, Job says, "The topaz of Ethiopia shall not equal it, neither shall it be valued with pure gold." (Job 28:19) The word translated "valued" in this verse is the Hebrew word calah. Here Job is saying that wisdom is beyond comparing against even jewels, and when weighed in the balance against wisdom, the finest jewels cannot equal its value.

The Amplified Bible adds "pause and calmly think about that" to each verse where Selah appears. When we see the word Selah in a Psalms or in Habakkuk 3, we should pause to carefully weigh the meaning of what we have just read or heard, lifting our hearts in praise to God for His great truths.

During these Selah moments, it is my desire that you will pause to allow Holy Spirit to reveal the truth of God and the lie of the enemy as you reflect on the information presented. You will be prompted to ask Holy Spirit, the Spirit of Truth, to show you His truth about the subject, and to shut out the other two voices: our human spirit and the enemy of our soul.

We know that Satan is the father of lies, but many of us are not aware of the fact that we can have blind spots and lie to

---

[2] https://www.gotquestions.org

ourselves unwittingly. We can't trust our own heart according to the scriptures: *"The heart is deceitful above all things, and desperately wicked: who can know it?" Jeremiah 17:9.*

Depending on Holy Spirit is of utmost importance in separating the "meat from the bones" and the truth from the lie. He will walk you through your journey of healing and wholeness as truth is being revealed, and you will experience the freedom His truth brings.

The title of this book was placed upon my heart in 2016. The 2010-2020 decade was prophetically very significant. At the beginning of the last decade, our church began to study the Hebraic roots of Christianity more intently. Our prayer was that God would grace us with the same anointing as the children of Issachar, *"which were men that had understanding of the times, to know what Israel ought to do" (I Chronicles 12:32, KJV).* According to the Hebrew calendar, the decade of the 2010s is recorded as the 5770s.

The Hebrew language is an ancient one that evolved from pictures. Each letter of the Hebrew alphabet represents not only a letter, but a prophetic picture and a number. For example, the number 70 in the Hebrew is the letter Ayin (ע). This letter is the symbol of the eye represented by the two yods at the top of the letter. (The yod's are also letters, each representing the number 10, as the Hebrew letters contain letters within the letter.) The two eyes speak of the choice we have, to see the negative or the positive.

According to the Hebrew calendar, Prophetically, the decade of the 2010s means to see, understand, witness and insight. As we gain God's understanding, witness, and insight, we will see farther than we have ever seen, and thus go farther than we have ever gone. 20/10 vision is sharper than 20/20 vision, causing things to come into better focus. The vision for this book was given to me during the previous prophetic decade to share in this current decade because it is all about focus and how we see things. How we saw our past experiences, and the emotions generated by how we saw it affects our ability to function in the present.

You will find other references to the Hebrew thought throughout this book for clarification to bring a deeper understanding of its meaning. "Hebrew thought views the world through the senses. (concrete thought) Concrete thought is an expression of concepts and ideas in ways that can be seen, touched, smelled, tasted, and/or heard."[3]

My prayer in writing this book is to help the reader gain a heavenly view regarding past hurtful experiences. The decade this book is being written in is a prophetic decade where that which we have seen, through the eyes of God will bring fruitfulness in our lives.

> "Moreover, the word of the Lord came to me, saying, Jeremiah, what do you see? And I said, I see a branch or shoot of an almond tree [the emblem of alertness and activity, blossoming in late winter]. Then said the Lord to me, You have seen well, for I am alert and active, watching over My word to perform it."
> Jeremiah 1:11-12, AMPC

---

[3] Jeff A. Benner, The Ancient Hebrew Language and Alphabet, Virtualbookworm.com Publishing Inc. 2004, College Station, TX 77842, p.2.

#You Too?

I once heard a well-known evangelist share about one of the times when she was ministering at the altar. A woman approached her for prayer and began to tell her what she was going through in her emotions. The evangelist's reply to her was, "You too!" That is not a typical response one would expect from a leader at the altar but in one way, it can be encouraging. The lie that the enemy of our soul wants us to believe is that we are the only one going through or have gone through what we are experiencing in our emotions. Believing that lie will cause us to hide behind a wall of shame or think something is wrong with us preventing us from seeking help.

I have a firsthand knowledge of what it feels like to experience emotional, spiritual, and even some mental abuse from those who claim to have a relationship with Jesus or called as leaders in the house of God. I've been a victim of rejection, jealousy, betrayal, false accusations, and the list goes on. I've also ministered to many others over the years who had been abused, mentally, emotionally, sexually, physically, and taken advantage of by those they trusted to be serving God.

I came to Christ when I was in my early twenties. My father was a PK (pastor's kid) and his unpleasant experience with the church caused him to make the decision as a young adult that his family wouldn't have anything to do with church. He never told us what he encountered, but we were told that this would be a decision we could make once we were adults.

When I made the decision to start attending church, I was very excited but naïve, and my expectations were very unrealistic. I was under the assumption that everyone had a special relationship with Jesus, especially those raised in church. That assumption set me up for many disappointing yet eye-opening experiences when it came to church and church people. I began to gain more and more understanding as to why my father came to the decision he made for our family; the woundedness he experienced as a child caused him to stray away from God in his adult life.

While doing street evangelizing, It was no surprise to me the many PKs I met who were no longer in church or following Christ, because of some of the hypocrisy, hurt, rejection, and unrealistic expectations placed upon them, along with other challenges they had experienced growing up in church. I have a special place in my heart for PKs who have lost their way because of not being properly equipped to navigate through their experiences.

When I came to know Christ, I had viewed church as a place of refuge from the day-to-day difficulties one may experience at work, in the marketplace, or even with family and relationships in general. I had no idea at first that I would encounter wolves in sheep's clothing. In studying God's Word, I read the words of

Jesus to His disciples in *Matthew 10:16: "Behold, I send you out as sheep in the midst of wolves. Therefore be wise as serpents, and harmless as doves."* I have embraced this approach to be aware, but to not allow that awareness to keep me from being and operating in who God has called me to be and do.

Imagine the shock I felt when I finally got the revelation that the Devil is a frequent visitor of church services, and will use people yielded to him, most times unknowingly, to wound others! When we read the Word of God, it becomes no surprise that the Devil could show up in church. For example, we read in the book of Job that he was bold enough to present himself before the throne of God:

> "Now there was a day when the sons of God came to present themselves before the Lord, and Satan also came with them. And the Lord said to Satan, 'From where do you come'? So Satan answered the Lord and said, 'going to and fro on the earth, and from walking back and forth on it.'"
> Job 1:6-7

A person with an experience is never at the mercy of one with an argument, that is why I believe what I have experienced, and the things God has showed me in the process, may help someone else.

Maybe your involvement in church has caused you to become disappointed, discouraged, or disillusioned about church and the people in it (what I call the 3 Ds). However, God tells us that He is able to flip the script and turn those stumbling blocks into stepping stones, leading to your destiny and purpose.

> "And everyone who was in distress, everyone who was in debt, and everyone who was discontented gathered to him. So he became captain over them. And there were about four hundred men with him."
> I Samuel 22:1

I call the people in this verse David's 3-dimensional army. They were hurt and wounded, but God was able to raise them up to be a victorious army. He is able to do the same today for those who will open up their wounds to Him and allow Him to pour in the oil and the wine.

I truly believed that by experiencing first-hand some of the hurtful situations a person may encounter in the church, he has enabled me to show others the way out, much like the man in the following story:

A Man Falls In A Hole[4]

This guy is walking down the street when
he falls in a hole.
The walls are so steep he can't get out.
A doctor passes by and the guy shouts out,
"Hey you. Can you help me out?"
The doctor writes a prescription,
throws it down in the hole and moves on.
Then a priest comes along and the guy shouts up,
"Father, I'm down in this hole, can you help me out?"

---

[4] http://westwing,bewarne.com/queries/story.html

> The priest writes out a prayer,
> throws it down in the hole and moves on.
> Then a friend walks by, "Hey Joe, it's me
> can you help me out?"
> And the friend jumps in the hole.
> Our guy says, "Are you stupid?
> Now we're both down here."
> The friend says, 'Yeah but I've been down here before
> And I know the way out.'"

Jesus is our only way out of whatever hole we might find ourselves in. My mission is to point you to Jesus who has been there and who is the way out. Looking at the ministry of Christ while He was on the earth, we will see that the "human" battles he encountered were primarily with the religious leaders. There was an established order that resisted the assignment He was on. News Flash! In the famous words of Jesus, *"If the world hates you, you know that it hated me before it hated you"* (John 15:18).

God has equipped me to help others to see beyond the hurt and see Jesus. Jesus, our High Priest came and had the human experience to connect us back to the Father.

> "Seeing then that we have a great High Priest who
> has passed through the heavens, Jesus the Son of
> God, let us hold fast our confession. For we do
> not have a High Priest who cannot sympathize
> with our weaknesses, but was in all points
> tempted as we are, yet without sin."
> Hebrews 4:14-15

Selah Moment: The enemy will always try to foster the lie in us that we are the only one going through what we are going through. He tries to clothe us in things like shame, guilt, condemnation, and lack of trust to keep us from reaching out for help. He isolates us with these thoughts to weaken us and to keep us bound. God's remedy for emotional healing can be found in *James 5:16a: "Confess your faults one to another, and pray one for another, that ye may be healed."*

List below any areas of hurt regarding your church experience to start your journey of refocusing to see the meat of God's word and not the bones of woundedness:

_____

_____

_____

_____

_____

_____

_____

_____

_____

"For the more we suffer for Christ,
the more God will shower us with His comfort
through Christ."
II Corinthians 1:5

Part 1
Why Were You Apprehended?

> "Not as though I had already attained, either were already perfect: but I follow after, if that I may apprehend that for which also I am apprehended of Christ Jesus."
> Philippians 3:12, KJV

The Apostle Paul was a man who was diversely educated and had achieved high ranking in the religious world (Philippians 3:4-6). Although his life reflected many accomplishments, he knew that he had not been perfected or had arrived. There was something missing. When he came to Christ, he wasn't satisfied with being saved. He knew he had been apprehended for a reason, because his life had been turned upside down! The religious blinders had been removed from his eyes, and he wanted to know why he was chosen by the Lord Jesus Christ. Revelation knowledge can be a powerful catalyst for our growth.

Revelation knowledge can be a powerful catalyst for our growth.

The general definition of "apprehend" is to: take into custody, arrest by legal warrant or authority; to grasp the meaning of, understand.[5] The Greek meaning is to lay ahold of so to make one's own.[6] In essence, what I hear the Apostle saying in this Scripture is, he needs to understand the purpose Christ apprehended him so he could follow that purpose and make it his own. You cannot maintain ownership of something you don't understand! If you don't understand it's nature, you will not be able to hold on to it.

You cannot maintain ownership of something you don't understand!

Why Did Jesus apprehend you? I encourage you to ask the Lord that question and not be satisfied until it has been fully revealed to you. You were apprehended by God for a purpose, and embracing this fact will send you in the right direction, similar to following a GPS device. To follow after something, your focus must be constantly focused on what you are following to not lose sight of it. What you focus on, is what you will draw towards. The Apostle Paul said that he would follow after that which he was apprehended so that he could apprehend it. This sounds much like the game of tag we played as children; someone tags you and you become "it." Paul had been tagged by the Lord, and so have you! He wasn't content in being apprehended but he wanted to apprehend what apprehended him ... and you should too.

In my years of learning and doing spiritual warfare, I strongly believe that the devil, being a spiritual being, has a somewhat limited foreknowledge of what God's preordained purpose is for our lives. He constantly tries to get us off focus

---

[5] https://www.Dictionary.com
[6] https://www.bibletools.org; Strong's #2638: Thayer's Greek Lexicon

with different distractions and detours. He is always on the job, so the way we can counteract his actions is to know *"that which we have been apprehended for."* In other words, we must be on the job of knowing our purpose. This will enable us to recognize and reject that which goes against God's purpose for us. When we know God's purpose for apprehending us beyond saving us, it becomes a powerful weapon to strengthen us and to aid us against the enemy's attacks. Exploring God's Perspective, God's Purpose and God's Plan will give you a greater understanding and further assist you in knowing and following after that which you were apprehended for.

Selah Moment: When I was a child, I had a dream that has stayed with me throughout my life. I was in a small room, and I could hear people crying around me outside of the room. People were coming to see me, and I was ministering comfort to them. In later years, it became clear to me that I was apprehended by the Lord to provide that comfort to others through the ministry of inner healing and deliverance. I experienced His emotional healing and deliverance for my life, and through that apprehension I am able to minister to others.

Ask the Holy Spirit to bring to your remembrance the indications that you may have received in the past through dreams, visions, or impressions giving indications of why you were apprehended by Christ. Write them down below, along with any current indicators.

_____

_____

_____

_____

_____

_____

_____

_____

"The Lord directs the steps of the godly. He delights
in every detail of their lives."
Psalms 37:23, NLT

Chapter 1
God's Perspective

Knowing God's perspective is knowing how He sees you. When you know and embrace how He sees you, you will begin to see yourself the same way, and have the motivation needed to apprehend that which you were apprehended for. One important way you can gain God's perspective on why you were apprehended is through His word:

> "But you are a chosen race, a royal priesthood, a dedicated nation, [God's] own purchased, special people, that you may set forth the wonderful deeds and display the virtues and perfections of Him Who called you out of darkness into His marvelous light."
> 1 Peter 2:9-10, AMPC

God says in His word that you were chosen and a valuable instrument for His work. An example of how the impact of being chosen can affect you can be related to the joy you felt as a child when you were picked to be on someone's team. You have been chosen by God because He sees value in you to be utilized for His Kingdom! The message and the mission are still true today. Each of us must go back to the cross where Jesus saw us and tell others about His love, as we see ourselves as God sees us.

For example, let's consider Saint Luke, who wrote the Gospel of Luke. The name *Luke* in the Hebrew means: Bringer of light and morning.[7] You will find plenty of revelation regarding the life, death, and resurrection of the Lord Jesus Christ in Luke's writing. He is credited for having a more complete history than the other gospels. He records twenty miracles of Jesus, as well as twenty-three parables, of which eighteen appear in his account. When reading the book of Luke, I always expect something to "dawn" on me that I hadn't seen previously. Luke, the "beloved physician," placed a special emphasis upon the kindness of Jesus towards women, the weak and poor, outcasts and those who were suffering.[8] The story of Zacchaeus, Luke 19:1-10, is a good illustration of the kindness of Jesus being shown towards an unlikely person according to society:

> Then Jesus entered and passed through Jericho. And, behold, there was a man named Zacchaeus who was a chief tax collector, and he was rich. And he

---

[7] https://charlies-names.com-Luke
[8] Hebrew-Greek Key Word Study Bible, King James Version, 1984, 1991 by AMG International Inc., page 2062.

sought to see who Jesus was, but could not because of the crowd, for he was of short stature. So he ran ahead and climbed up into a sycamore tree to see Him, for He was going to pass that way. And when Jesus came to the place, He looked up and saw him, and said to him, "Zacchaeus, make haste and come down, for today I must stay at your house." So he made haste and came down, and received Him joyfully. But when they saw it, they all complained saying, "He has gone to be a guest with a man who is a sinner."

Then Zacchaeus stood and said to the Lord, "Look, Lord, I give half of my goods to the poor; and if I have taken anything from anyone by false accusation, I restore fourfold." And Jesus said to him, "Today salvation has come to this house, because he also is a son of Abraham, for the Son of Man has come to seek and save that which is lost."

In verse 3, the story states that Zacchaeus was a man of small stature, which limited his ability to see in the midst of the crowd. This would appear to be obvious to the casual observer. However, we could also view his stature from a different angle; he may have been judged small in the eyes of others because of his position as a tax collector, which brought him ill-gained wealth (verse 2). The response from the crowd in verse 7 confirmed the overall attitude of the people towards Zacchaeus when Jesus invites him for a visit. They murmured amongst themselves as to why Jesus would want to

> *The judgments projected upon us by others can cause us to view ourselves in the same way.*

fellowship with someone they had judged and labeled a sinner. The judgments projected upon us by others can cause us to view ourselves in the same way. To quote the inspirational words from the comedian W.C. Fields: "It isn't what they call you, it's what you answer to."

Zacchaeus did not answer the call of judgment by others or allow their labelling to deter him from his mission: he "sought to see Jesus, who he was" (verse 3). When he chose to climb the sycamore tree, he put himself in position to see Jesus and not the bones collected based upon the opinions of others. He chose to follow the cloud of the presence of Jesus and not the crowd!

The sycamore tree is considered a symbol to Israel of regeneration because of this particular event. *Regeneration* means spiritual renewal and revival, restoration, and the concept of being born again.[9] Not only was he able to see Jesus clearly, but he made himself visible and available for Jesus to see him (verses 5, 6).

In verse 7 we see another way in which Zacchaeus placed himself in the right position by; facing his accusers; humbling himself, repenting for his past transgressions and offering restitution fourfold. This humbling act by Zacchaeus ushered the way for his visit with Jesus. When we come before the Lord in repentance, it sets the stage for us to be reset and redirected. In verse 9, Jesus declared salvation for his household and Zacchaeus's position as a son of Abraham because as a Jew working for a foreign country oppressing them, he was viewed as a traitor and considered an outsider.

In the Jewish culture, names are purposely given to children that speak prophetically of their destiny. The name Zacchaeus

---

[9] https://www.merrian-webster.com

in Hebrew means clean, pure. Zacchaeus was not walking in his prophetic God ordained destiny with his current occupation. Tax collectors were viewed as sinners because they worked for the Roman government utilizing dishonest methods when collecting the taxes from the people. The circumstances surrounding his life so far, had hidden his true identity and purpose for being in the earth.

We can also gain God's perspective on how He sees us when we spend quality time with Him in prayer. Prayer is a two-way dialogue. God is always speaking, and He will speak to us about how He sees us as we go to Him on a regular basis. Below is a brief summary from a children's book written by famed Christian author, Max Lucado, *You are Special; A story for Everyone*: [10]

> The story is about a town consisting of wooden people called Wemmicks, carved by a woodworker named Eli, who lived on the top of the hill. The Wemmicks were all different in appearance, but were carved by the same carver. They did the same thing every day giving each other stickers. Each Wemmick had a box of golden stars and gray dots. The ones who were pretty, had smooth paint and talented were given stars. The ones that received stars would feel so good that they would try and do something else to get another star. However, those who didn't meet the criterion, were given dots. One such person was named Punchinello, he had dots all over him. When he tried to do what the others did to earn stars, he failed and was surrounded by the other Wemmicks and given

---

[10] *You are Special; A story for Everyone*, Max Lucado, Crossway Books, 2011, pg. 45.

dots. He had so many dots that he was reluctant to go outside, and when he did, he was given more dots for no reason but because he had so many dots already! He was taunted by the wooden people that he wasn't a good Wemmick and he deserved more dots and in turn, he started to say the same about himself. He felt more comfortable and hung around other Wemmicks who had a lot of dots like himself.

One day, he met a girl named Lucia who didn't have any stars or dots on her. The people tried to give her stickers, but they would just fall off. Punchinello decided he wanted to be like Lucia, without stickers. He asked her how did she do it? She told him that she went to see Eli the woodcarver every day and sat in his woodshop. Punchinello went to see Eli and was surprised that Eli knew his name. Eli reminded him that he had made him and that he was special. He also told him not to be concerned what the other Wemmicks said about him because they were wooden just like he was. Eli shared with him that Punchinello matter to him because he made him, and he didn't make mistakes. When Eli was asked why the stickers didn't stick on Lucia, this was the woodcarver's reply: "Because she decided that what I think is more important than what they think. The stickers only stick if you let them. You've got a lot of marks. For now, just come to see me every day and let me remind you how much I care."

When we spend time with our maker, he will give us His perspective, how He sees us. Go see Him every day, so you can see the value He sees in you and how much He cares.

Selah Moment: Have you ever driven on the highway behind a semitruck and observed a sign posted on the back trailer: "If you can't see my mirrors, I can't see you." This sign is posted for the safety of the other vehicles on the highway. The driver of the big rig is letting other drivers know they must place themselves in a position of visibility for the truck driver. Otherwise, the driver will be in the trucker's blind spot. The sign reminds us to look for the truck's mirrors, so that we are visible to the truck driver. In Zacchaeus' case, he climbed the tree to look for Jesus, God's mirror of Himself, and became visible and validated.

Allow Holy Spirit to show you the source and origin of any labels attached to you by others or yourself, promoting feelings of unworthiness and other false messages, hindering your ability to see yourself how God sees you. Write down those lie based labels, renounce all agreements with them and ask Him to show you how God sees you.

_____

_____

_____

_____

_____

_____

_____

Is There Any Meat on the Bones?

___

___

___

___

___

___

___

___

___

___

___

___

___

"How precious are your thoughts about me, O God.
They cannot be numbered!"
Psalms 139:17, NLT

Chapter 2
God's Purpose

The word *purpose* is defined by Merriam-Webster as, "The reason why something is done or used, the aim or intention of something, feeling of being determined to do or achieve something, the aim or goal of a person."[11]

God may speak about our purpose to us through personal prophecy received from others who we trust to hear from God. There are two specific scriptures found in the book of I Timothy that make references to the prophetic used in the speaking of purpose:

> "Do not neglect the gift that is in you,
> which was given to you by prophecy with the laying
> on of the hands of the eldership."
> I Timothy 4:14

---

[11] https://www.merriam-webster.com/dictionary/purpose

> "This charge I commit to you, son Timothy,
> according to the prophecies previously made
> concerning you, that by them you may wage the
> good warfare."
> I Timothy 1:18

You were born into this life with a unique and divine purpose. Knowing your divine purpose, the reason you were born and the reason you were born again, will help you stay on course. It becomes a weapon to use against the warfare you may encounter from the mind, the flesh, others, or the enemy.

Prophecies are to be made, reviewed, and weighed by leadership when it doesn't come directly from them. A good way to war a good warfare is to write down the prophetic word(s) and make them a matter of prayer for God's preparation, timing, and direction.

The following are some important reasons why knowing and embracing your purpose will aid you on your journey in fulfilling God's purpose.

Knowing God's purpose will cause you to seek out where it can be developed.

There are numerous times when people are considering a church home that they may have their own shopping list of amenities. I have witnessed many people who seek for a place of worship for creature comfort and not to prepare them for what God has purposed for their lives. To borrow and apply a quote from humorist Finley Peter Dunne used by other ministers, "Jesus didn't just come to comfort the afflicted but, He also came to afflict the comfortable!" In the book of Ephesians, we discover how the church is structured to prepare us to fulfill His purpose for us:

> "Now these are the gifts Christ gave to the church:
> the apostles, the prophets, the evangelists, and
> the pastors and teachers. Their responsibility is
> to equip God's people to do his work and build up
> the church, the body of Christ."
> Ephesians 4:11-12, NLT

When you are in the right church, your leadership will be given revelation by God to confirm your purpose or calling and He will also use them to develop your gifts and talents. I experienced that at Evangel Christian Churches during the time I was being trained as an Elder. God spoke to me while in prayer one morning during my time of journaling and said He had called me to, "shepherd His sheep." I never told anyone what was spoken to me that day. I didn't go out to purchase ministry business cards or begin to encourage people to address me as "Pastor." Instead, I waited for confirmation from the one God called me to serve, the one who watches for my soul (see Hebrews 13:17). It so happened, that one day, as I was speaking with Bishop Jerry about another matter, out of the blue he said that God spoke to him while he was in prayer and told him that I was called to be a pastor. He was used by God to not only confirm my calling but to groom me for it!

Just like Jesus had a purpose for apprehending Zacchaeus when he selected him out of the crowd, he also has a purpose for you. Like Zacchaeus, He may have apprehended you out of the crowd of worldly influences, from family, friends, co-workers or even your church congregation to fulfill His purpose through you. The good news is, you have been apprehended or you wouldn't be reading this book!

Knowing God's purpose helps you to stay on course.

The state of Florida is a peninsula with many beautiful beaches. There is also a specific kind of water current called rip currents that can occur near beaches with breaking waves. It is a strong, localized, and narrow current of water that moves directly away from the shore, cutting through the lines of breaking waves, like a river running out to sea. Rip currents are especially dangerous because they move perpendicular to the shore and can be strong enough to sweep the strongest swimmer away from the shore quickly. The current does not pull you under, it just sweeps you out to sea quickly if you are caught in one. The best way to come out of a rip current, besides staying calm and/or yelling for help, is to swim parallel to the shore.

When we find ourselves being pulled away from God's purpose, whether it is from hurt, loss, disappointment, sins of the flesh, etc., we should stay parallel to our purpose by staying in fellowship, reading the word, prayer, worship and staying accountable to leadership. During these times, purpose is your shore to swim parallel to. I remember how Bishop Jerry would quote Revelation 2:5, *"Do your first works"* to help those who had been somehow pulled away from purpose to become realign with their purpose.

Let your season of personal struggles be a life lesson, and not a life sentence!

It is not about how you feel, but what you need to do to survive those seasons where you find yourself experiencing challenges to your faith that have tried you, or have pulled you in the wrong direction. I call these "seasons of insanity." These are times when our minds rent out space to the enemy, and sweep us away with the current of deception. Let your season of personal struggles be a life lesson, and not a life sentence!

Knowing God's purpose gives you more determination.

The Oxford Learners Dictionary defines the word *determination* as, "A quality that makes you continue trying to do or achieve something that is difficult: the act of finding out or calculating something. the act of officially deciding something."[12] Knowing our purpose gives us a feeling of determination to do or achieve something. There is a goal in view, along with an intended or desired result, aim, and end. You are being purpose-driven and not force-driven. When you do something with purpose, you will do it with determination. The following story is an example of how knowing your purpose will give you determination. In an article written for Charisma Magazine, author and pastor Dutch Sheets relates a story told in the *Pentecostal Evangel* by J.K. Gressett, who wrote about a man named Samuel S. Scull, who settled in the Arizona desert with his family:[13]

> One night a fierce storm struck with rain, hail, and wind. At daybreak, feeling sick and fearing what he might find, Samuel went to survey their loss.
>
> The hail had beaten the garden into the ground; the house was partially unroofed; the henhouse had blown away and dead chickens were scattered about. Destruction and devastation were everywhere.
>
> While standing dazed, evaluating the mess, and wondering about the future, Samuel heard a stirring in the lumber pile that was the remains of the henhouse. A rooster started climbing up and

---

[12] https://Oxfordlearnersdictionaries.com
[13] https://charismamag.com/spiritled-living/purposeidentity/dutch-sheets-do-you-need-an-infusion-of-hope/

continued until he had mounted the highest board in the pile. The old rooster was dripping wet, and most of his feathers were blown away. But as the sun came over the eastern horizon, he flapped his bony wings and proudly crowed. When the morning sun appeared on the horizon, that beat-up, featherless rooster-amidst all the chaos and devastation-still crowed, announcing the beginning of a new day. Why? Because he knew what he was purposed to do.

One interesting note about roosters is that their physique has been used as weathervanes for many centuries because the shape of their tail is perfect for catching the wind. The roosters purpose gave him the determination he needed to rise above the damage the wind from the storm caused. We won't allow the challenging winds to control us when we walk in determined purpose.

Allow what seems to be a setback be God's setup for a comeback!

The awareness of God's purpose for your life will give you determination, as the light of the Son before you will empower you to rise up and go forward beyond what the storms of life may present. Allow what seems to be a setback be God's setup for a comeback!

Knowing God's purpose helps you to recognize Him in and through the process.

While you are on your journey toward walking in the purpose God has for you, you will experience His processing. Processing involves a series of actions, carried out in a specific order to achieve a particular result. It involves change. This is illustrated by the natural process of growth we experienced as children that changed us physically, emotionally, mentally, and socially.

Changing things grow and growing things change! Being processed can, at times, become very uncomfortable and even overwhelming. The growth process can be a time of testing that can deter us if we are not aware of God's purpose. My husband once had a dream in which the Lord spoke to him and gave him a simple truth: "Where you *want* to be is easy, where you *ought* to be is harder." That is the process. It's important to see God involved in every step of the process as part of His divine plan to have you arrive at your purpose.

Viewing the processing of the Lord in our lives as seasons, and not challenges, can sometimes keep us from feeling overwhelmed, powerless, trapped, helpless, etc. When we think of seasons, we think of eventual change, therefore, we aren't looking for the place we are currently in to last forever. You are only passing through and don't have to file a homestead exemption! You can embrace a familiar passage found throughout Scripture, "And it came to pass" for a prophetic declaration that where you are now is not where you will always be.

Changing things grow and growing things change!

Seeing that the process you are going through is to prepare you for your purpose will give you peace that surpasses all understanding (see Philippians 4:7). Having the peace of God allows you to focus on the promise and not the process. Having God's peace in the midst of the process will almost have a numbing effect similar to what I experienced during minor surgery on my thumb. When the doctor numbed my thumb, he promised me that as he began to cut into it, I would feel the pressure, but I would not feel the pain. You will feel the pressure of the process, however focusing on God's purpose for your life will allow you to recognize the process, making the pressure less intense. During your time of being processed, you may feel like throwing in the towel. If you decide to do that, the towel may be returned to you with God's reminder that His purpose determines the process.

> "I have told you these things, so that in Me you may have [perfect] peace and confidence. In the world you have tribulation and trials and distress and frustration; but be of good cheer [take courage; be confident, certain, undaunted]! For I have overcome the world. [I have deprived it of power to harm you and have conquered it for you.]"
> John 16:33, AMPC

Selah Moment: We can see in our previous story concerning Zacchaeus, how elevation allows us to see Jesus because it puts us at an arial advantage point to see above our challenges. He sought higher ground and Jesus stepped in and said in *Luke 19:5b, "for today, I must abide in your house."* When you are in the midst of God's processing for purpose, seek His face and Jesus will step in and make His purpose known to you.

Take a moment to ask Holy Spirit to show you anything from the past or present preventing you from experiencing God's peace and list them. Invite the presence of Jesus into each one of them and write down next to them what thought or impression you may have received or sensed to assist you in feeling His peace.

_____

_____

_____

_____

_____

_____

_____

_____

"Who has saved us and called us with a holy calling, not according to our works, but according to His own purpose and grace which was given to us in Christ Jesus before time began,"
II Timothy 1:9

Chapter 3

God's Plan

God's plan for our lives is not always visible to us at first. A plan is basically a detailed proposal for doing or achieving something; an intention or decision about what you are going to do, and how you are going to do it. For example, the Apostle Paul didn't know entirely what the plan God had for him entailed, but he made himself available *after* his encounter with Jesus on the road to Damascus (see Acts chapter 9). The whole plan or council of God at that time was not revealed, but Paul was given step-by-step instructions, which he followed to fulfill God's plan for apprehending him and His plan for him. He encountered many obstacles and successes on his journey, yet he stated that his former life was nothing compared to what he had received walking in the plan of God:

> "But what things were gain to me, these I have counted loss for Christ. Yet indeed I also count all things loss for the excellence of the knowledge of Christ Jesus my Lord, for whom I have suffered the loss of all things, and count them as rubbish, that I may gain Christ."
> Philippians 3:7-8

The Ultimate Plan of God Involves All

God's ultimate plan for us all can be found in the prayer that Jesus taught His disciples, recorded in Matthew chapter 6 and Luke chapter 11: "Thy Kingdom come, thy will be done on earth as it is in heaven." We must be born again to see the Kingdom (John 3:3). To enter God's Kingdom, we must be born of water and of the Holy Spirit (John 3:5). As we grow in grace, and in the knowledge of our Lord and Savior Jesus Christ (II Peter 3:18), we are to go out and make disciples (Mark 16:15-16). God's plan is that we become representatives of His Kingdom here on earth.

God's Plan for Us Is Constantly Unfolding

It's important that we do not allow the unexpected challenges of doing life distract us or detour us from the plan God has ordained for our lives: *"The LORD directs our steps, so why try to understand everything along the way?" Jeremiah 10:23, NLT*

There is a familiar Scripture quoted in the Body of Christ for encouragement. Sometimes I wonder if people who embrace it really understand the circumstances surrounding the time when God spoke that word to the children of Israel given by the Prophet Jeremiah to share.

> "For I know the plans I have for you,"
> says the LORD,
> "They are plans for good and not disaster,
> to give you a future and a hope."
> Jeremiah 29:11, NLT

The children of Israel had been carried away, and were in the midst of Babylonian captivity that lasted for seventy years. It was a dark time for God's people, and yet He spoke this word indicating His plans of hope and prosperity in the midst of that darkness. Oh, how that must have spoken life to their situation, knowing His plan for the future! Even In the midst of chaos, God can make His plan known and put it into action in our lives. In the midst of our captivity, God's plan will speak hope and future to us! God's plan must be larger in our hearts than the challenges we encounter, because He is well able to move in the midst of it all!

When God's plan for our lives have been embraced, we can rest assured of the end result.

During the construction of a house, road, bridge, or building, you can see things that are missing, scattered, and appear out of place. There's a lot of dust, noise and other activities occurring at that time. In the midst of the construction, something is being shaped, formed, and improved until completion of the project. When God's plan for our lives have been embraced, we can rest assured of the end result.

> "Being confident of this very thing, that he which
> hath begun a good work in you will complete it
> until the day of Jesus Christ."
> Philippians 1:6

> "The LORD directs the steps of the godly. He delights in every detail of their lives. Though they stumble, they will never fall, for the LORD holds them by the hand."
> Psalms 37:23-24, NLT

Following the Plan of God Is a Walk of Faith

Faith causes us to trust God's hand when we don't know His plan. Romans 10:17 states, "So then faith cometh by hearing, and hearing by the word of God." The Old and New Testaments record the story of how Abraham (Abram at the time), stepped out in faith on the initial word God spoke to him without knowing what God was planning.

Faith causes us to trust God's hand when we don't know His plan.

> "Now the LORD had said to Abram: "Get out of your country; from your family, and from your father's house, to a land that I will show you."
> Genesis 12:1

> "By faith Abraham obeyed when he was called to go out to the place which he would receive as an inheritance. And he went out, not knowing where he was going. By faith he dwelt in the land of promise as in a foreign country, dwelling in tents with Isaac and Jacob, the heirs with him of the same promise; for he waited for the city which has foundations, whose builder and maker is God."
> Hebrews 11:8-10

God's Plan Will Do a Work in Us Before He Executes it Through Us

God's plan for us can be like putting the pieces of a puzzle together. As the many different shapes of the puzzle are being connected, the hidden picture is slowly being revealed.

There are things we encounter externally in our lives that help build us internally.

It takes a lot of time, patience, and determination, as the pieces are being assembled. There's some sorting that takes place, while pieces of the same color and pattern are being collected and separated into piles. The external border of the puzzle is formed, starting with the corners, followed by the middle pieces being assembled together to compose the final picture. Likewise, God's plan for our lives does an internal work in us during our journey of faith to completion.

There are things we encounter externally in our lives that help build us internally. We gain strength in the struggles as the sorting takes place, separating our flesh from the spirit, fortifying us for His plan. The plan of God will do an intimate work in us, *In-to-me-see*. This internal work builds character in us. Character is the collective mental and moral qualities that make a person who they are. The original meaning of the word *character* was the name given to a sculptor's tool; the forming chisel used in developing a statue. The chiseling away to form the character of Christ in us may sound painful, but God is more interested in our character than our comfort!

Our gifts and talents may advance us, but our character is what keeps us. Our reputation is the external that others see, but our character is who we are when no one is looking. God's plan for us will literally turn us inside out, so that what is on the outside is also

God is more interested in our character than our comfort!

a true reflection of the inside. When we have been strengthened from the inside out, we are better able to withstand the external pressures we may encounter following God's plan.

The Plan of God Won't Always Line Up With Ours

Our plans are usually based on finite thoughts compared to God's. *"My thoughts are nothing like your thoughts," says the LORD. "And my ways are far beyond anything you could imagine"* (Isaiah 55:8, NLT). King David was declared by God as being a man "after His own heart." David loved God and wanted to show forth that love by building Him a permanent temple to house the Ark of the Covenant, which represented the presence of God in the Old Testament. In his last words of instruction to the people, and especially to his son Solomon, he expressed that plan:

> "David rose to his feet and said: "My brothers and my people! It was my desire to build a Temple where the Ark of the LORD's Covenant, God's footstool, could rest permanently. I made the necessary preparations for building it, but God said to me, 'You must not build a Temple to honor my name, for you are a warrior and have shed much blood."
> 1 Chronicles 28:2-3, NLT

> "Every part of this plan," David told Solomon, "was given to me in writing from the hand of the LORD."
> 1 Chronicles 28:19, NLT

When the ultimate plan of God is continuously in our view, to allow His Kingdom in the earth to be established through us, our plans will always synchronize with His.

> "You can make many plans, but the LORD's
> purpose will prevail."
> Proverbs 20:24, NLT

> "Commit everything you do to the LORD.
> Trust him, and he will help you."
> Psalms 37:5, NLT

> "We can make our own plans, but the LORD
> gives the right answer."
> Proverbs 19:21, NLT

Selah Moment: After living several years in Florida, my husband and I decided to buy another home. We were looking for a newer home, something built within the last ten years. Little did we know that God's plan for our next home was that it would be built from the ground up; a home where we would be the first inhabitants! That idea had never entered our minds, but God's plan went beyond what we had purposed to do. That is what is meant by *1 Corinthians 2:9, NLT: "No eye has seen, no ear has heard, and no mind has imagined what God has prepared for those who love him."*

Take a moment and allow Holy Spirit to bring to your remembrance those plans you've had, where you experienced God going beyond what you expected. List those examples of God's faithfulness. Take this time also to write down and release to Him any of your plans that have not come into fruition and allow Him to bring you peace.

_____

_____

_____

_____

_____

_____

_____

God's Plan

"I know, LORD, that our lives are not our own.
We are not able to plan our own course."
Jeremiah 10:23, NLT

Part 2
Is it a Family Affair?

Our family of origin plays a vital role in how we view the situations and circumstances we face in relational matters. Family members rely on each other for emotional, physical, mental, and economic support. Families are the primary source in shaping a person into an adult. You had no voting rights regarding your family, but it is important to be aware of the circumstances that brought you into this world and your family dynamics. Your future began to be shaped while you were in your mother's womb. Your family is your emotional frame of reference from where most of your core beliefs about yourself, others, and God come from. The list below gives several examples of situations that will impact us emotionally during our early development which may have a significant effect on our adult life.

- Circumstances around your conception: Were you unplanned (labeled an accident), were you born out of wedlock, or a result of rape?

- Did your mother abort a child before you were conceived or considered an abortion while carrying you?
- What was the emotional state of your mom during the pregnancy?
- Did you or your mother experience any birthing trauma?
- Were you born breeched or pre-mature?
- Are you a twin, triplet, etc.?
- Were you the sex your parents wanted?
- Were you raised by both biological parents, single parent, or an extended family member?
- Were you adopted or raised in the foster care system?
- Were you separated from your family for extended lengths of time e.g., hospitalization or summers away from home?
- What was your family size; small, medium, or large?
- Were your parents/guardians there for you emotionally or physically. Did you feel loved, accepted, validated, or supported by them?

Your answers to the above questions will give you an indication of how you perceive the world around you and the people in it. Another important family dynamic is your position in the family and the role played contributed to the functioning of the family unit.

Your position in the family refers to where you fit in the birth order; first born, middle child, youngest child or only child. Each role has a different set of personality traits with variations depending upon the spacing between births, culture, blended families, etc. The following is a brief summary of these four main positions and general tendencies taken from *The Birth Oder Book* by Dr. Kevin Leman:[14]

- *First Born Child*: Perfectionist, reliable, conscientious, a list maker, well organized, hard driving, natural leader, critical, serious, scholarly, logical, doesn't like surprises, a techie.
- *Middle Born Child*: Mediator, compromising, diplomatic, avoids conflict, independent, loyal to peers, has many friends, a maverick, secretive, used to not having attention.
- *Youngest born*: Manipulative, charming, blames others, attention seeker, tenacious, people person, natural salesperson, precocious, engaging, affectionate, loves surprises.
- *Only Child*: Little adult by age seven, very thorough, deliberate, high achiever, self-motivated, fearful, cautious, voracious reader, black and white thinker, talks in extremes, can't bear to fail, has very high expectations for self, more comfortable with people who are older or younger.

There are different roles that are taken on by the members of the family that also contribute to the functioning of the family. Depending on how healthy the family is will determine to what extent these roles are carried out and whether they are helpful or hurtful. A healthy family will consist of support, love and caring for other family members along with open communication, making each other feel important, valued, respected, and loved.

---

[14] Dr. Kevin Leman, *The Birth Order Book: Revised and Updated*, New York, NY, MJF Books, 1985,1998, 2009, page 18.

Families with constant conflict, abuse, addictions, neglect, etc., are labeled dysfunctional and specific roles are also created within the family to keep it functioning. (Dysfunctional families can be compared to opening the windows when it is freezing weather outside and turning the furnace up trying to heat the room.) These families will seem normal to their members because of the continual exposure and constant reinforcement. Below is a list of common family roles with a brief description taken from an article found in the Innerchange.com:[15]

- *Hero*: This is the "good" responsible child. This person is a high achiever, carries the pride of the family, and he/she overcompensates to avoid looking or feeling inadequate. Sometimes the hero lacks the ability to play, relax, follow others, or allow others to be right.

- *Rescuer:* The rescuer takes care of others' needs and emotions, and problem-solves for others in the family. This person doesn't realize that sometimes helping hurts. He/she also lives with a lot of guilt and finds it challenging to focus on him/herself.

- *Mediator:* This person does the emotional work of the family to avoid conflict. He/she acts as a buffer, and does it in the name of helping others, although it may be for his/her needs. This can be a healthy role depending on how the person mediates.

- *Scapegoat/Black Sheep*: This is the person the other family members feel needs the most help. Usually this is the family member in need of treatment or in treatment. The person may have strengths such as a sense of humor,

---

[15] https://www.innerchange.com/parents-resources/family-roles/ ©2022

a greater level of honesty, and the willingness to be close to his/her feelings.

- *Switchboard:* He/she keeps track of what's going on by being aware of who is doing what and when. However, this person focuses on everyone else's issues rather than his/her own.

- *Power Broker:* This person works at maintaining a hierarchy in the family with him/herself at the top. His/her safety and security with life depends on feeling in control of the environment around him/her.

- *Lost Child:* He/she is obedient, passive, and hidden in the family trauma. He/she stays hidden to avoid being a problem. However, he/she lacks direction, is fearful in making decisions, and follows without questioning.

- *Clown:* The clown uses humor to offset the family conflict and to create a sense that things are ok. The person has a talent to readily lighten the moment but he/she hides his/her true feelings.

- *Cheerleader:* The cheerleader provides support and encouragement to others. There is usually balance in taking care of his/her own needs while providing a positive influence on those around him/her.

- *Nurturer:* This person provides emotional support, creates safety, is available for others, and can be a mediator. He/she focuses on having and meeting emotional needs, usually in a balanced manner.

- *Thinker:* The thinker provides the objective, reasoning focus. His/her strength is being able to see situations in a logical, objective manner. However, he/she may find it difficult to connect emotionally with others.

- *Truthteller:* This person reflects the system as it is. Other members in the family might be offended or avoid the truthteller because of the power of truth he/she holds.

Sometimes a child will take on the characteristics of more than one role, depending on the perceived needs of the family. How you entered this world, your family of origin, or whichever role(s) you may identify with and what position you held in the family, will assist you in understanding how it has affected you as an adult. You may also be able to recognize and understand some of the above-mentioned tendencies in the behavior of others. This awareness could possibly decrease the frequency of viewing some of the negative behaviors you've experience from others, as a personal attack, affecting you emotionally.

You may have felt at times that you were programmed because of the influences of your family. You may have found yourself repeating some of the negative cycles, patterns, and behaviors seen in your family. The good news is that, with Jesus, the script that was written from those influences can be flipped! Those influences that work against you and God's purpose for your life can be eliminated. The following passage of Scripture gives us an excellent example of how it can be possible:

> "Jabez was honorable above his brothers; but his mother named him Jabez [sorrow maker], saying, Because I bore him in pain. Jabez cried to the God of Israel, saying, Oh, that You would bless me and enlarge my border, and that Your hand might be with me, and You would keep me from evil so it might not hurt me! And God granted his request."
> I Chronicles 4:9-10, AMPC

- He was born with negativity spoken over him (a curse) and was blamed because of the birthing trauma his mother experienced, something he had no control over.
- He didn't allow these circumstances to restrain him from living his life so honorable that it exceeded his brothers.
- He chose not to allow the negativity of the past to direct his path in life. He called upon the only one that could help him, (his creator) and petitioned Him for his future. His actions were so profound that it warranted God's attention, God interrupted the recording of the genealogy for the sons of the tribe of Judah, (The tribe Jesus was to come out of) to bring attention to his story.
- He not only prayed for the natural things, but he also prayed for God's divine protection from the possibility of evil that would want to follow him because of the circumstances surrounding his birth.

Jabez's mother gave him a name out of her pain. The healing of hurts received from parental figures from our childhood will enable us to separate their pain from what is truly ours. The relationship Jabez had with the Lord superseded the effects of the family situation he was born into.

Selah Moment: The petition Jabez brought before the Lord consisted of the ability to break through the negativity of his past and set a victorious path for his future. It contained four major parts that I believe can be applied to those things working against us from our family of origin:

1. God's blessings; 2. God's enlargement beyond the present; 3. His presence with us; and 4. His protection from evil, which would try to capitalize on our past.

Ask Holy Spirit to show you and list below any hurtful areas pertaining to your family of origin and their possible effect on your adult life. Apply the prayer of Jabez for each one listed.

> *The petition Jabez brought before the Lord consisted of the ability to break through the negativity of his past and set a victorious path for his future.*

_____

_____

_____

_____

_____

_____

_____

"I sought the Lord, and He heard me, and
delivered me from all my fears."
Psalms 34:4

Chapter 4
Parents and Others in Authority

We began our interaction with our parents/guardians in a helpless state. We were dependent upon them for our very existence. We learned that there were certain ways we had to respond to maintain a state of well-being with them.

Our parents/guardians will have the greatest impact on how we interact with authority figures; they are the first authorities we encounter growing up, and our first example of the authority position. If that experience included painful unresolved memories, if unresolved, they will affect our adult life in many ways.

How we related to our parents or other key authorities in our life growing up, whether good, bad, or indifferent, is how we will relate to the authorities in our lives as adults, including God. These relationships will spill over in the church world and will have an impact of how we receive, respond, or perceive those in leadership. Below are some of the indicators that you may have unresolved issues with one or both of your parents/guardians:

- You avoid or fear any type of contact with your parents/guardian.
- You experience physical symptoms when you are around your parents such as stomachaches, backaches, headaches, nervousness, sweaty palms, etc.
- You feel like you cannot count on relationships.
- You battle with shame and guilt-often feeling a need to apologize.
- You tend to put your own emotional needs last.
- You are very critical of yourself.
- You constantly need validation.
- You feel responsible for your parent's/guardian's behavior.

For the past thirty years, I have had the opportunity to do personal ministry with church members who have been wounded emotionally by parents, teachers, coaches, doctors, church leaders, law enforcement, etc. There were things done to them, spoken to them, and spoken over them as a child by people in authority having a lasting impact on them emotionally. How they viewed what happened and the message they received will carry over into their adult life. Many of the conflicts they were currently having could be traced back to the type of parenting style they received.

It is very important to identify the style of parenting you experienced growing up, as it will give you more of an understanding of how you see God and other authority figures. There are four traditional and four modern parenting styles classified by psychologist according to early childhood development specialist Anastasia Moloney in her article found in "The Tot."[16] These parenting styles are listed with a short summary:

Traditional Parenting

- *Authoritative:* Considered the most effective. Holding high expectations, but still "understanding." Create structure and routine in both the parent's and child's day. Having consequences when rules are broken. Healthy and open line of communication. Parents speak to their children without judgements. Helps child to understand and respond to the world around them.
- *Neglectful:* Identified as the most harmful types of parenting. Not meeting child's emotional or physical needs. The home may not be a safe space for the child. The child may often be left alone. Lack of involvement in the child's life such as school.
- *Permissive:* This is also known as indulgent parenting. Responsive, but not demanding. Avoid confrontation, causing them to be lenient. Very loving and nurturing. Inconsistent rules. Seeks to be child's best friend.
- *Authoritarian:* This style of parents is also known as strict parenting, meaning the parent can be very

---

[16] https://www.thetot.com/mama/parenting-styles/

demanding but not always responsive. Limited open dialogue between parent and child. Children are expected to follow a strict set of rules. Child is offered limited choices or decisions about their own life. Use punishment to teach a lesson. Reserve the amount of warmth and affection they show.

Modern Parenting

- *Free-range*: Parenting from a free-range perspective is to allow and encourage your child as much freedom and independence that is appropriate for their age and development. Provide children with autonomy, self-reliance, and responsibility early and often. Allowing kids to have unsupervised time to explore their environments. Teaching kids a realistic acceptance of personal risks. Free-range parents believe they are giving their children their childhood back.

- *Helicopter*: Helicopter parenting is a coined term for "overparenting." This means the parent is involved in a child's life in a way that is over-controlling, over-protecting, and over-perfecting. Parents begin with good intentions to protect their child. The parent often solves the problem for a child. Child relies on the parent to solve the issue.

- *Paranoid:* This parenting style is controlled by worry and fear that something might happen to their children. Parents not allowing their children to join in activities due to safety concerns. Children's outdoor and creative play is restricted due to anxieties.

- *Positive:* The focus of positive parenting is to establish love and connection and to resist the temptation to be punitive, but rather guide with control and empathy. Parents who are committed to regulating their own emotions. Parent shows unconditional love. Parent focuses on establishing a connection before the correction or behaviors. Limits are set, but they are set with empathy.

You may have experienced more than one of the described styles above, or a different style from each parent. The style that seems to be more dominate in your mind and emotions will be the one having the most affect upon you. For example, if you were the product of a neglectful parenting style, you may feel a sense of abandonment often in your relationship with God when challenges come. You may also find yourself unconsciously drawn towards relationships that neglect your needs. These feelings of neglectfulness by God and others will trigger those unresolved hurts from the past, intensifying the emotions in the present.

There was one ministry session I had with a gentleman I'll call Logan. Logan grew up in a single parent household where his mother was very neglectful of his need for support. When he was in middle school, he had a teacher who appeared to single him out for discipline, even though other students were committing the same violation. He felt very picked on and unsupported by his mother who never came to the school to assess the situation.

After Logan became a parent, whenever his son would complain to him about an incident at school, he was there defending his son vehemently, even if his son was at fault. He always sided with his son believing that the teacher was always being unjust towards his son. His heart was to be there for his son because his mother wasn't there for him, but instead, he enabled his son's negative behavior and disrespect for authority. His good intentions had the opposite outcome because Logan overcompensated and overreacted in matters regarding his son and school officials. He reacted more from his emotions than objectively to the situations because he was blinded by his own unresolved issues with his mom not defending him, and against his teachers because he felt he was not treated fairly by them.

How we see Father God is connected to how we related to our parents/guardian. The father, especially, is a prototype of God and if he was absent emotionally or physically, it will impact our ability to trust God. How we relate to Father God influences how we relate to one another and other leaders in our lives.

Selah Moment: Our parents are imperfect human beings as we all are, and capable of making mistakes. The Lord is able to heal us with His love and show us our true identity in Him along with His purpose for us being born into the family we were. We can find hope for healing from His promise found in *II Corinthians 6:18: "I will be a Father to you, and you shall be my sons and daughters..."* God is a perfect replacement for our imperfect parents!

Which of the above parenting styles are you able to identify with? Allow Holy Spirit to show you how that particular style has affected your relationship with God, others, and your church family. List the memories below, the emotions attached and forgive all involved.

_____

_____

_____

_____

_____

_____

_____

_____

_____

"Although my father and my mother have forsaken me,
yet the Lord will take me up
[adopt me as His child]."
Psalms 27:10, AMPC

Chapter 5
In The House But Not in the Family

When we are aware of the dynamics in our family of origin, and how we were raised, a light can be shed on the reactions we have concerning relational challenges involving our church family. It has been my experience in the various churches I was a part of, that there were some personalities in the congregation that either reminded me of a parent or some other close family member. We are often drawn towards the familiar that can trigger unresolved issues.

We are often drawn towards the familiar that can trigger unresolved issues.

The Bible gives many stories about different families and the dynamics involved. There is one story found in the book of Luke that affected me personally. This story really pulled on me emotionally for some time and changed my life and my relationship with the Lord dramatically. Being the middle child, I have the tendency to look for the justice in things and in this particular story, I felt a sense of unfairness was rendered. To be totally honest, and at the risk of being judged, I was stuck for a season because my sense of fairness was based on the influences of the family I grew up in as a child. The story I am referring to is the parable of the prodigal or lost son found in Luke Chapter 15:11-32. I will give some of the verses below to outline the story and share with you why it affected me the way it did.

> "Then He said: (Jesus) 'A certain man had two sons. And the younger of them said to his father, 'Father, give me the portion of goods that falls to me.' So he divided to them his livelihood. And not many days after, the younger son gathered all together, journeyed to a far country, and there wasted his possessions with prodigal living. But when he had spent all, there arose a severe famine in that land, and he began to be in want. (vs. 13-14)
>
> But when he came to himself, he said, 'How many of my father's hired servants have bread enough and to spare, and I perish with hunger! I will arise and go to my father, and will say to him, 'Father, I have sinned against heaven and before you, and I am no longer worthy to be called your son. Make me like one of your hired servants.' (vs. 17-19)
>
> "But the father said to his servants, 'Bring out the best robe and put it on him, and put a ring on his hand and sandals on his feet. And bring the fatted

calf here and kill it, and let us eat and be merry; for this my son was dead and is alive again; he was lost and is found.' And they began to be merry. Now his older son was in the field. And as he came and drew near to the house, he heard music and dancing. So he called one of the servants and asked what these things meant. And he said to him, 'Your brother has come, and because he has received him safe and sound, your father has killed the fatted calf.' But he was angry and would not go in. Therefore, his father came out and pleaded with him. So he answered and said to his father, 'Lo, these many years I have been serving you; I never transgressed your commandment at any time; and yet you never gave me a young goat, that I might make merry with my friends. But as soon as this son of yours came, who has devoured your livelihood with harlots, you killed the fatted calf for him.'" (vs. 22-30)

The overall point of the story may have been obvious to most, especially when you are able to view it objectively, however I was viewing it subjectively because I identified with the elder son due to my unhealed childhood hurts. Holy Spirit showed me that the reason I was affected so much by this particular story was because I really saw myself in him. Feeling that an injustice had been committed brought some hidden anger in me to the surface. God used the stirring this story caused in me to show me how I was serving Him out of works and not out of relationship. One day Holy Spirit spoke to me and told me that our relationship was like railroad tracks, paralleled, and not touching, therefore not connected. There was a lack of intimacy that I thought I had, but there were some areas of my heart that were closed to Him due to the influences of my childhood. When there is an absence of love, fear takes up residence, especially the fear of intimacy because it becomes the fear of the unknown.

Here are some of the dynamics of my family of origin that can further illustrate why I identified emotionally with the elder son. I came from a large family of nine. My father was an alcoholic and my mother was very ill; she died when I was thirteen years old. Both parents were emotionally unavailable to me as a child. There was no affection and I was never told that I was loved. My basic needs were met, I was not physically abused or neglected, but I always felt like I was alone and just existing. Whatever attention or positive enforcement I received was based on the things I did and how well I did them. I especially spent a great deal of time around my mother attending to her. I was the oldest girl at home when she passed, so I took on a lot of the household responsibilities. I grew up as a servant to my parents and not a daughter. This story revealed to me how I was relating to Father God in the same way I did with my parents and helped me to learn what true intimacy was with the Father.

My identity was wrapped up in what I did and not who I was. The revelation of who I was came forth as I sought intimacy with the Father. One thing I observed when I was attending one of the mainstream denominational churches is the fact that quite a few members held on to positions for many years. There would be some conflict if there was the slightest possibility that someone else may be given their position. Hurt feelings occur when our identity is in the position we hold and we can begin to feel threatened, jealous, unappreciated, and rejected.

The elder brother in our story was always there being the good son, but it was obvious that he saw himself more as a servant as he indicated in verse 29 along with his list of good deeds. In verses 17-19, the younger brother saw being a servant in his father's house was less of a position to what he held as a son. The younger brother approached his father as a son asking for his inheritance. He had to have some confidence of his position in the family and with his father for him to ask for the portion of his inheritance that was his after his father died. In essence, by his request, he was saying, you are living too long, I can't wait any longer, it's my money and I want it now!

The anger rose in the elder brother because he related to his father by his works and didn't see himself being rewarded for staying home and being faithful to his father. I call this the stay home run-away syndrome. His body was at home, but his spirit wasn't. He was in the house but not in the family. His brother did what he might have been fearful of doing because when we have a servant's mentality, there is a deep fear of rejection if we do anything unacceptable. The younger brother's decision to venture away from home is an indication that he was not satisfied with his current living condition. I had a couple of brothers who would run away from home frequently, but I was too fearful. I was very unhappy inside just like them. My body was at home, due to the fear of rejection or punishment, but my spirit was gone. I was just going through the motions, but my heart was not always in what I did.

The elder brother didn't go in to celebrate the return of his younger brother because his focus was on himself. Works can be used as a hiding place from true intimacy. Everyone was in the house celebrating, connecting with one another in love, while he was on the outside looking in. Obviously, he had some things he wanted to have, but didn't ask for it (see verse 29). When there is a lack of intimacy, there is the tendency to not allow our needs to be known. This may foster an expectation that others should intuitively know what we need. The elder son was also lost; he was lost emotionally in the house! There are many people hurting in God's house not feeling connected to the family of God.

I have observed what I call the *elder brother syndrome* in many churches. New people come in and if they are shown too much attention by the pastor or leaders, a jealousy begins to surface among those that have been there awhile. Those who have not established that intimacy with the Father and look only to man for validation will fall into this snare of the enemy.

This story is a wonderful reflection of the heart of Father God towards His children. In verse 20 of our story, the father saw the younger son approaching while he was afar off which could indicate that he may have been doing this frequently looking and hoping for his son's return any day: "And he arose and came to his father. But when he was still a great way off, his father saw him and had compassion, and ran and fell on his neck and kissed him."

The following is an excerpt summary of the song by Mark Altrogge titled "I'm Forever Grateful" and I think it truly illustrates the heart of the Father:[17]

> You did not wait for me - to draw near to You
> But You clothed Yourself with frail humanity
> You did not wait for me - to cry out to You
> But You let me hear Your voice calling me
> I'm forever grateful ... that you came to seek and
> save the lost

The same love and compassion shown to the younger son, was also shown to the elder son in *verses 31 and 32*: "And he said to him, 'Son, you are always with me, and all that I have is yours, It

---

[17] Altrogge, Mark, "I'm Forever Grateful," ©1986 by People of Destiny International

was right that we should make merry and be glad, for your brother was dead and is alive again, and was lost and is found."

The father left the party to see about him and to let him know how important he was to him by acknowledging their bond and the fact that everything he had was his. He also took the time to explain the importance of him celebrating the return of his brother to the family. The elder son was blinded to the fact that he was loved by his father, not for his works but because of relationship, to the point that he couldn't appreciate the fact that his younger brother was home safe. This kind of self-focus could open the way for narcissism when there is a disregard for the needs or feelings of others and a strong sense of entitlement because you feel you deserved better.

Relating to the Father only through our works places the focus on ourselves and limits our ability to experience real intimacy in our relationship with Him. We can find ourselves on the treadmill of perfectionism, fear of failure, fear of rejection, self-rejection, shame, guilt, false responsibility, etc. It also sets us up for hurt from feelings of anger, betrayal, disappointment, and/or rejection because we feel used, unappreciated, or taken for granted. Just like the father in our story, Father God doesn't allow our human failures to separate us from His love. It wasn't our works that afforded us salvation so we shouldn't rely on our works when it come to our relationship with the Father.

> "For by grace you are saved through faith, and that not of yourselves; it is the gift of God, not of works, lest anyone should boast."
> Ephesians 2:8-9

Selah Moment: *"The Lord is like a father to his children, tender and compassionate to those who fear Him, for He knows how weak we are; He remembers we are only dust" (Psalms 103:13-14, NLT).* Embracing this Scripture has helped me tremendously in my quest for more intimacy with the Father. My father was very strong when it came to discipline so I had a constant fear of punishment. Therefore, I had an unhealthy fear of God. This fear caused me to hide behind my works rather than seek intimacy with Father God. When I embraced His unconditional love and compassion towards me in spite of my imperfection, it removed barriers I had built up in my heart hindering intimacy.

> "There is no fear in love; but perfect love casts out fear because fear involves torment. But he who fears has not been perfect in love."
> I John 4:18

Do you sometimes have difficulty embracing God's love and acceptance because of past failures? List those areas below and invite the presence of Holy Spirit to show you the heart of the Father towards you in those areas. Receive His love and forgiveness and forgive yourself.

_____

_____

_____

_____

"But God showed His great love for us by sending
Christ to die for us while we were still sinners."
Romans 5:8 NLT

Chapter 6
Curses

I grew up in a household where my parents were very reluctant to share information regarding our family history. They held fast to the practice of not allowing children in the same room when adult conversation was being held. This practice kept a lot of our family secrets from past generations to remain hidden. Most things I learned later in life from speaking with older relatives brought more understanding about some things I experienced which unknowingly affected my life and the decisions I made as an adult.

You can find in the Old Testament a list of various curses, especially in the book of Deuteronomy chapter 28:15-68. These curses are areas of opposition against the will of God, which consequently will set in motion harm or punishment affecting the future of the person or nation being cursed.

Out of these biblical curses, there is a particular set of curses that are passed down through the generations known as ancestral curses. This is the passing down of sinful behaviors (rebellion against God) that repeats in the next generation. If not broken, curses can continue to the third and fourth generations.

> "Keeping mercy for thousands, forgiving iniquity and transgression and sin, by no means clearing the guilty, visiting the iniquity of the fathers upon the children and the children's children to the third and the fourth generation."
> Exodus 34:7

These are doors to the enemy opened by the actions of previous generations. They can affect some of the things we encounter, especially if you find yourself experiencing cycles, patterns, and behaviors in your family tree. The following are a few examples of curses that can travel through the generations if not addressed:

- Divorce, breakdown of marriages and family alienation
- Addictions
- Chronic sickness, especially heredity or those without clear medical diagnosis
- Poverty or continued financial insufficiency when the income seems sufficient
- Family history of suicide, homicide, early deaths, abortions,
- Adultery
- Unforgiveness, grudges, anger

- Illegitimacy
- Repeated miscarriages and other female problems
- Mental Illness or emotional breakdown.
- Calamity, mayhem, accident prone

The Online Etymology Dictionary defines a curse as follows: Late Old English *curs;* "a prayer that evil or harm befall one; consignment of a person to an evil fate." Middle English *cursen,* from Old English *cursian* "to wish evil to; to excommunicate,"[18] This definition of a curse shows that when a curse is operating in a person's life because of past generational activities, that curse directs their path through consignment and excommunication. Both consignment and excommunication are about putting a person in a place where they will be forgotten or in an unpleasant situation. A curse is a place where there is an absence of God due to rebellion against the will and word of God.

It is very important for Christians to have a knowledge of curses. It is one of the common ways the enemy uses to block our view and allows us to be influenced to respond in a way that is contrary to the Word of God. These generational curses can lead us down a path of sin that we had no intention of following because of our love for God and desire to serve Him. The following verses excerpted from the 20th chapter of Genesis, tells the story of the unrepented sin of the father from the previous generation and its effect upon the son in the following generation.

> "And Abraham journeyed from there to the South, and dwelt between Kadeh and Shur, and stayed in

---

[18] https://www.etymonline.com

> Gerar. Now Abraham said of Sarah his wife, 'She is my sister.' And Abimelech king of Gerar sent and took Sarah."
> Genesis 20:1-2

> "Then Abimelech said to Abraham, 'What did you have in view, that you have done this thing?' And Abraham said, 'Because I thought, surely the fear of God is not in this place; and they will kill me on account of my wife.'"
> Verses 10-11

This next portion of Scripture shows a repeat of the above scenario with Abraham's son Isaac:

> "So Isaac dwelt in Gerar. And the men of the place asked about his wife. And he said, 'She is my sister'; for he was afraid to say, 'She is my wife,' because he thought, 'lest the men of the place kill me for Rebekah, because she is beautiful to behold.'"
> Genesis 26:6-7

This same king basically, had the identical confrontive conversation with Isaac as he did with his father Abraham previously. The Scripture doesn't tell us in chapter 20 whether Abraham ever repented after he was confronted by King Abimelech; after making excuses, he went on in verse 12 to explain that Sarah was really his sister from his father's side of the family but not his mother's, trying to justify his lie. Abraham's behavior makes it apparent how the generational curse he created set the spiritual pathway for Isaac to follow the same pattern of sin.

Here is a personal example about the curse of anger.

As I shared previously, my father was an alcoholic and sometimes when he was drunk, he would be in a very angry mood. We would experience his anger directed towards family members. I became fearful and angry about his treatment of us, and I criticized and judged him in my heart many times. As an adult, because I wasn't shown as a child how to manage my anger in a healthy manner, I found myself projecting my anger in unhealthy ways.

One evening as I was pulling into my driveway, after a very stressful day on my job, Holy Spirit spoke to me in such a gentle loving way: "Now don't go in there and take your anger and frustration out on your children." At that moment, I received deliverance. The word spoken to me brought conviction and awareness that I was following the same generational curse experienced by my father who was a victim of his own father's anger as a child. I noticed anger trying to manifest in my children and after taking it before the Lord in prayer, I heard, "When it's broken in you, it will be broken in them." Our knowledge of generational ancestral curses will not only provide freedom for us but for the generations that come after us.

Our knowledge of generational ancestral curses will not only provide freedom for us but for the generations that come after us.

Jesus became cursed, so that we can be blessed. *"Christ has redeemed us from the curse of the law, having become a curse for us (for it is written; "Cursed is everyone who hangs on a tree;" (Galatians 3:13).* Below are sample prayers that can be used to break the power and effect of any ancestral generational curses that may apply to your life.

Suggested Prayer to break Ancestral Curses: Father, I come to you in the name of Christ Jesus and in the power of His blood to break the curse of _____ over my family along with the power and affects, holds, yokes, and bondages, and command the blood line to be purged in the name of Christ Jesus. Amen

For those curses you don't know about, I suggest you pray: Father, I come to you in the name of Christ Jesus and in the power of His blood, praying that every curse of iniquity coming down through the family line on the father's side and the mother's side, ten generations backwards and forwards be broken in the name of Christ Jesus.

Another type of curse I want to bring to your attention is what are known as those self-imposed curses. This particular curse involves inner vows of judgments made regarding our parents/guardians. God's general principle regarding judging, established in his Word, sets in motion the law of reciprocation. This involves the response given to an action in a way that corresponds or is somehow equivalent to that action.

> "Judge not, that you be not judged."
> Matthew 7:1

This is similar to what was learned earlier regarding ancestral curses, the fact that it affects the person's future. The only difference is that this curse is self-imposed and only affects the person making the judgment. This curse involves the negative inner vows or judgments made towards our parents/guardians called a Bitter Root Judgment. When did your parent/guardian first fall off their pedestal? At what age did you discover they were not perfect? Likely during this time, inner vows, called Bitter Root Judgments, would start to take residence.

> "Looking carefully lest anyone fall short of the grace
> of God; lest any root of bitterness springing up cause
> trouble, and by this many become defiled."
> Hebrews 12:15

When we judge, there is a defilement or contamination that occurs in us due to the activation of God's principle of sowing and reaping. A Bitter Root Judgment has an expectancy with it that whatever area you judged your parent/guardian in, will be the same area you will reap in your character or your relationships with others in authority.

> "Do not be deceived, God is not mocked;
> for whatever a man sows, that he will also reap."
> Galatians 6:8

Judging our parents/guardians negatively causes us to dishonor them in our hearts thus setting in motion the promise given in the fifth commandment:

> "Honor your father and mother, which is the first
> Commandment with promise."
> Ephesians 6:2

> "Honor your father and your mother, as the Lord
> has commanded you, that your days may be long,
> and that it may be well with you in the land which
> the Lord your God is giving you."
> Deuteronomy 5:16

The promise is that when we honor our parents/guardians all will go well with us. However, the opposite will occur when we dishonor them. Making a judgment or inner vow against our parent/guardian is not just about dishonoring them, we are dishonoring God's choice for your parents. You may think your issue is with your parents because you can see them and interact with them directly. However to dishonor them by judging them is to say that God made the wrong decision in giving you the parents He did. God always sets us up for blessing and not failure.

Honoring your parents is not sanctioning any wrong done towards you; they will answer to God for their actions. Your responsibility is to forgive them, allow God to heal your emotions, and honor the office of authority God gave them in your life. Some examples of Bitter Root Judgments we may have made inwardly as a child:

- A female might say, "I'll never let a man treat me like my father treats my mother."
- A male might say, "When I get grown, no woman is going to control me like my mother did my father or me."
- "I'm not going to raise my children the way I was raised, I can do a better job than my parents."
- My parents are stupid, dumb, ignorant, etc.
- "I'm going to be more successful than my parents."
- "I'm not going to act like my father/mother."
- "I will not allow anyone to hurt me like my parents hurt me."
- "Nobody's ever going to tell me what to do, I'm going to always do what I want to do."

> "Whoever curses his father or his mother, His lamp
> will be put out in deep darknes."
> Proverbs 20:20

The "deep darkness" will be like a cloud over your life when it comes to relating to authorities and serve as fertile ground for the judgment seed. The seed sown starts out small, but if it continues to be unchecked, it grows deep roots and bears fruit that shows up in our adult life. The law of sowing and reaping guarantees that we will be held accountable for the judgments made towards our parents/guardians. The following are a few examples of the fruit that manifests in our adult life from childhood Bitter Root inner vows:

- You change jobs or/and churches frequently.
- You tend to be scrutinizing, judgmental and critical towards authority.
- You feel like striking back or telling others off who are in authority.
- You often challenge the decisions of your boss and other authorities.
- Women have trust issues with their husbands, men have trust issues with their wives.
- You often feel singled out and harassed by those in authority.
- Whatever gender of the parent/guardian you had issues with is the same gender you will have trouble submitting to as your authority.
- You tend to overreact to constructive criticism, adjustments, or corrections by authority figures especially when it is directed towards your talents, gifts, and abilities.

It is very important that we identify any Bitter Root inner vows made towards our parents/guardians; much of the hurt we experience in our lives and in church will most likely come from leadership because of the expectations we have placed upon them to treat us in a certain way. God uses leadership as His representatives in the earth to grow us up as adults to fulfill His plan for our lives. Sometimes these authority figures will remind us of our parents/guardians. If there are any judgments made towards our first authorities, unhealed, it will affect how we perceive and receive from them. We must be able to filter out what is true and what is the lie of the enemy when it comes to the authorities in our life.

> "Let every soul be subject to the governing authorities. For there is no authority except from God, and the authorities that exist are appointed by God. Therefore whoever resists the authorities resists the ordinance of God, and those who resist will bring judgment upon themselves."
> Romans 13:1-2

Prayer to release yourself from any Bitter Root Judgements/inner vows: Father, I come to you in the name of Christ Jesus and the power of His blood, asking your forgiveness for dishonoring the parents you have chosen for me by making Bitter Root Judgments or inner vows towards them. I also pray that you break the power and effect of this curse and its expectancies over my life and heal every wound that opened the door for the seeds to be planted in the name of Christ Jesus, Amen!

Selah Moment: *"And he will turn the hearts of the fathers to the children, and the hearts of the children to their fathers, lest I come and strike the earth with a curse" (Malachi 4:6).* Our God is a God of relationship. He sent His son Jesus to reconcile us back to Him so we can have fellowship with Him. The enemy of our soul attempts to use our unhealed childhood wounds as a divisive weapon to hinder our relationship with Father God and one another. His power is canceled when we do the following: confess our hurts, repent, forgive self and others, ask and receive God's forgiveness.

Pray and ask Holy Spirit to reveal specific Bitter Root Judgments and/or inner vows with their instances. Forgive the offender and ask for forgiveness for self.

_____

_____

_____

_____

_____

_____

_____

_____

_____

Is There Any Meat on the Bones?

"For you did not receive the spirit of bondage again
to fear, but you received the Spirit of adoption
by whom we cry out, 'Abba, Father.'"
Romans 8:15

Part 3
Is It Really About You?

We live in a culture that encourages self-promotion. Sometimes the greatest weapon that the enemy uses against us is ourselves. We give him power when our measurement of a situation is based upon our perception of how, what is, or has happened, impacts us personally. Using the character of our lives as a measurement for the lives of others, will always be a source of disappointment and hurt.

Self-preservation is internally built within us, due to the fall of man in Genesis 3, and is activated when we feel limited or threatened in any way. This tendency to defend ourselves can motivate us to respond in the flesh and not in the Spirit of Christ. When we become self-focused, we can be consumed emotionally and blinded spiritually. When this happens, the appeasement of our flesh will rise above our desire to please God.

Please note that this is not advocating the unhealthy, dysfunctional practice of neglecting yourself or your needs for the needs of others. It is not the promotion of living a life of denial that submits you to many forms of abuse, which can affect you mentally, emotionally, physically, or even spiritually.

It is learning how to apply God's Kingdom principles as taught in the scriptures, which allows you to see beyond yourself and apply these principles to your situation, preventing you from getting stuck, emotionally, mentally, and spiritually.

Bible scholars teach about the principle or law of *first mention* as found in Scripture. This is where an important word or concept occurs for the first time, and is mostly found in the book of Genesis, the book of beginnings. As we look at the following verses from the book of Genesis, we will be able to see through the law of first mention, the first example of the entrance of sin into the world and get a perspective on strategies used to entice us. The first couple; Adam and Eve, were manipulated with words spoken by the serpent:

> "Now the serpent was more cunning than any beast of the field which the Lord God had made. And he said to the woman, "Has God indeed said, 'You shall not eat of every tree of the garden'?" And the woman said to the serpent, "We may eat the fruit of the trees of the garden; but of the fruit of the tree, which is in the midst of the garden, God has said, 'You shall not eat it, nor shall you touch it, lest you die.'"
> Genesis 3:1-3

The question we should ask ourselves is: Why did the serpent go to the woman instead of the man, even though the man received his instructions directly from God and the man and woman were together at the time? I believe the answer can be found as we look at their beginnings.

> "And the Lord God formed man of the dust of the ground and breathed into his nostrils the breath of life; and man became a living being."
> Genesis 2:7

However, when we look at the creation of the woman, we see a difference:

> "And the Lord caused a deep sleep to fall on Adam, and he slept; and He took one of his ribs and closed up the flesh in its place. Then the rib which the Lord God had taken from man He made into a woman, and He brought her to the man. And Adam said:
> "This is now bone of my bones and flesh of my flesh;
> She shall be called Woman,
> Because she was taken out of Man."
> Verses 21-23

The tree of good and evil could be symbolically viewed as a choice between the Spirit and the flesh. Before, Adam and Eve didn't have to choose: ". . . everything was very good." (Genesis 1:31). After partaking of the fruit of the tree, they were presented with the knowledge and necessity to choose. Our fleshly choices will contaminate our spiritual growth and the temptation to accept the bait of self-focus and self-protection is always present.

The serpent approached the flesh of Adam to carry out his plan of attack. Our flesh gives the enemy access to us. When we look at this first encounter with the enemy recorded in the book of beginnings, it shows a pattern that we can learn from, illustrating some of the repeated strategies of the enemy.

- *The lack of knowledge of or misinterpretation of God's word.*

    God's instructions to Adam in *chapter 2 of Genesis, verses 16-17 were: "…of every tree of the garden you may freely eat: but of the tree of the knowledge of good and evil, you shall not eat, for the day you eat, you shall surely die."* Nothing was said about them touching it. There was a personal contribution made by Eve to the instructions given by God that added a more restrictive tone to the subject. Adding our own slant to God's word can lead us down the wrong path, the path of disobedience and deception.

- *The doubt and unbelief of God's word.*

    Genesis 3:4, "Then the serpent said to the woman, 'You will not surely die.'" Declaring God's word is one of the main weapons we have available to deflect any attacks of the enemy (Ephesians 6:17). Jesus modeled this truth by quoting the Word when the devil tried to tempt Him at the end of His forty-day fast in the wilderness (Matthew and Luke chapter 4). When God's word is tainted with doubt and unbelief, it will lessen its effectiveness in our lives and provides more room for the flesh to rule.

    > *Adding our own slant to God's word can lead us down the wrong path, the path of disobedience and deception.*

- *Personalizing the situation encouraging possessiveness.*

    Genesis 3:5, "For God knows that in the day you eat of it your eyes will be opened and you will be like gods, knowing good and evil." When the serpent personalized God's instructions to Adam and Eve, it became implied as God's attempt to withhold something that would benefit them. There are a couple of spirits introduced subtly: Fear of lost empowerment and rejection by God for withholding the tree from them. At this point, their focus was more on the tree than on God. They became obsessed with the tree. The lesson here is: What you focus on you will gravitate toward. Obsession leads to possessiveness and possessiveness invites control. As with Adam and Eve, any dialogue the serpent has with us will appeal to our flesh, which craves self-promotion. This was his declaration before Satan was evicted from Heaven as recorded in *Isaiah 14:14b*: *"I will be like the Most High."*

> *When God's word is tainted with doubt and unbelief, it will lessen its effectiveness in our lives and provides more room for the flesh to rule.*

> *Obsession leads to possessiveness and possessiveness invites control.*

- *The lust of the flesh and eyes to justify.*

   Genesis 3:6, "So when the woman saw that the tree was good for food, that it was pleasant to the eyes, and a tree desirable to make one wise, she took of its fruit and ate. She also gave to her husband with her, and he ate." When the flesh begins to take control in our decision-making process, justification of what we are about to do strengthens our case of how right or reasonable it will be to do it. When we justify our actions, the spirits of pride, rebellion, and denial will take up residence in our souls to affect our mind, will and emotions. *1 John 2:16 tells us, "For all that is in the world-the lust of the flesh, the lust of the eyes, and the pride of life-is not of the Father but is of the world."*

Knowing and correctly applying the Word of God will keep you from the deception of the enemy. The Word can subdue our flesh so we can be led by the Holy Spirit. The Word can expose when our flesh is trying to take control and bring adjustment, correction, and realignment.

> "For the word of God is living and powerful, and sharper than any two-edged sword, piercing even to the division of soul and spirit, and of joints and marrow, and is a discerner of the thoughts and intents of the heart."
> Hebrews 4:12

Genesis 3:20 says, "And Adam called his wife Eve, Because she was the mother of all living." Not only can we see Eve as a representative of the flesh, but also as the bearer of the seed for future generations. The enemy's aim is not just towards you; his desire is also to affect the coming generations.

Giving into the demands of the flesh will cause you to sacrifice your future and the upcoming generations on the altar of the now!

> "And I will put enmity between you and the woman, and between your seed and her seed; he shall bruise your head, and you shall bruise his heel."
> Genesis 3:15

Adam and Eve were the first fruits of the future generations of mankind. We are the first fruits of the future generations of our families. The decisions we make must go beyond ourselves to take in consideration what effect it will have on future generations. Giving into the demands of the flesh will cause you to sacrifice your future and the upcoming generations on the altar of the now! When you are stuck in your flesh because of your woundedness, you are unable to see beyond yourself and unable to influence others for the Kingdom of God.

> "[That is] because the mind of the flesh [with its carnal thoughts and purposes] is hostile to God, for it does not submit itself to God's Law, indeed it cannot."
> Romans 8:7, AMPC

Is it really about you? The enemy wants you to think that so your reaction will come from your fleshly nature. Jesus told His disciples in *Luke 9:23b;* *"If anyone desires to come after Me, let him deny himself, and take up his cross daily, and follow Me."* The Apostle Paul stated in I Corinthians 15:31 that he "dies daily." Dying daily refers to the Kingdom of God's principle of dying to self-promotion and the influences of the flesh.

Selah Moment: There are certain indicators in our speech, when used frequently, can reflect the fact that we are personalizing the situation too much. Do you tend to use "I" statements along with your opinion in addressing most situations you are emotional about? For example, "*I* don't understand why they did this to me because I wouldn't have done it to them." "If it were me, *I*...." "This is the way *I* would have handled it." "This is what *I* think, feel, should have happened." "*I* can't see...."

You will notice in the above verses of both Genesis and Ezekiel, the same personal pronouns of *you, your,* and *I* being used as a prelude to fleshly decisions. Doing so takes the focus off of God and His Word, and places it on self-promotion. Personalization can be a subtle type of control, which can cause one to feel out of control when the outcome of the situation is different than what we personally believed should have happened. Expectations based on our own personal view sets us up for disappointment and leads to hurt, anger, rejection, etc.

Allow the Holy Spirit to show you any situations or incidences in your life where the expected outcome was based on your personal thought or feeling of what should have happened. Ask Him to show you God's truth and renounce any negative emotions attached to it.

_____

_____

_____

_____

"Therefore, [there is] now no condemnation (no adjudging guilty of wrong) for those who are in Christ Jesus, who live [and] walk not after the dictates of the flesh, but after the dictates of the Spirit."
Romans 8:1, AMPC

Chapter 7
Make No Bones About It!

I have very close friends who prefer to eat fish with the bone in. They seem to get so much pleasure from the challenge of separating the meat from the bones. It is almost like they are on an important mission to get the bones as clean as possible. When my husband gives them fish that he caught, they prefer he not remove the bones. I, on the other hand, welcome my husband's filet knife! As I had determined from a child, after experiencing being poked and almost choked by fish bones, the risk is too high, it involves too much work, and adds unnecessary time to the meal. I chose the path of less resistance in this instance because of my past experiences and the inconvenience I anticipated. I had no patience for the process. My friends may have experienced the same things that I had, but they view picking through the bones as a welcomed task, and are not discouraged by what might or could happen in the process.

Looking at this on the emotional level, many of us have experienced wounds from the past that can cause us to take these two approaches to the challenges we encounter. The above example could be contrasted as that of one who has been healed of emotional hurt and one who has not experienced healing. A person who has gone through the healing process, when they encounter the possibility of being wounded again, is able to see beyond the potential hurt. When necessary, this person is willing to receive more healing. Those, however, who have not experienced God's healing power from past hurts will tend to allow fear of being reinjured to cause them to build up sinful self-protectors, hindering emotional and spiritual growth. This protective mechanism encourages a person to build up walls within their heart, promoting isolation. Isolation causes them to feel overwhelmed with a sense of dread, because they see themselves as the only one who can resolve the issue before them. These feelings can lead them to attempt to find ways to avoid or escape confrontation.

They may justify their avoidance with spiritual sounding phrases like; "I don't feel lead." Or "I don't feel a release in my spirit." Or maybe not so spiritual phrases like, "let sleeping dogs lie." The problem with sleeping dogs is that they can wake up at an inopportune time and bite you with anger, regret, resentment, depression, addictions, etc.

There is an example of the two approaches found in the book of Numbers chapter 13. Moses sent the twelve spies to spy out the land of Canaan God promised them. Ten saw the potential trouble, while two saw the potential victory.

> "Now they departed and came back to Moses and Aaron and all the congregation of the children of Israel in the Wilderness of Paran, at Kadesh; they brought back word to them and to all the congregation, and showed them the fruit of the land. Then they told him, and said: "We went to the land where you sent us. It truly flows with milk and honey, and this is its fruit. Nevertheless the people who dwell in the land are strong; the cities are fortified and very large; moreover, we saw the descendants of Anak there."
> Numbers 13:26-28

> "But the men who had gone up with him said, 'We are not able to go up against the people, for they are stronger than we.' And they gave the children of Israel a bad report of the land which they had spied out, saying, 'The land through which we have gone as spies is a land that devours its inhabitants, and all the people whom we saw in it are men of great stature. There we saw the giants (the descendants of Anak came from the giants); and we were like grasshoppers in our own sight, and so we were in their sight.'"
> Numbers 13:31-33

Personalization will cause us to only see ourselves on the scale of how big the problem is and not on the scale of how big our God is. The ten spies were looking through their own eyes and using themselves as not only a measurement compared to the giants but also a judge of how the giants saw them based on that same measurement. The ten became weighed down with the obstacles and became overwhelmed, seeing only their fears in the equation of things. Joshua and Caleb didn't give the power to the obstacles described; they knew that God had brought them there and that God was able to give them the land. They knew that with God on their side, the giants would be unprotected and in their hands.

> *Personalization will cause us to only see ourselves on the scale of how big the problem is and not on the scale of how big our God is.*

> "Then Caleb quieted the people before Moses, and said, 'Let us go up at once and take possession, for we are well able to overcome it."
> Numbers 13:30

> "But Joshua the son of Nun and Caleb the son of Jephunneh, who were among those who had spied out the land, tore their clothes; and they spoke to all the congregation of the children of Israel, saying: 'The land we passed through to spy out is an exceedingly good land. If the LORD delights in us, then He will bring us into this land and give it to us, "a land which flows with milk and honey." 'Only do not rebel against the LORD, nor fear the people of the land, for they are our bread; their protection has departed from them, and the LORD is with us. Do not fear them."
> Numbers 14:6-9

Selah Moment: It's very important to know your personal approach when you are faced with challenges that stretch you beyond your comfort zone. How you approach challenges will determine how they will affect you emotionally and may rob you of your promised future. We can approach life's challenges with a victim mentality or that of a victor through Christ Jesus. A victim may face their challenges wanting to be rescued, finding someone to blame, or living in a fantasy world. A victor will confront the situation head on, having experienced the faithfulness of God in past hurtful experiences. Whatever approach you choose, you can't allow the "bones" to keep you from the "meat." We have already been forewarned in the scriptures that we will encounter those things that may wound us when we are in Christ. *"Yes, and all who desire to live godly in Christ Jesus will suffer persecution," (II Timothy 3:12).*

Do you tend to see the challenges you face mostly with a perceived possibility of being wounded in some way? Ask Holy Spirit to show you incidences from your past, and to help you to see those situations with Jesus in it.

_____

_____

_____

_____

_____

_____

Is There Any Meat on the Bones?

_____

_____

_____

_____

_____

_____

_____

_____

_____

_____

_____

_____

_____

"I have told you all this so that you may have peace in me.
Here on earth, you will have many trials and sorrows.
But take heart because I have overcome the world."
John 16:33, NLT

Chapter 8
Error of Entitlement

Those who have been mistreated or disrespected will harbor and exhibit a sense of entitlement. They will start to believe that they deserve better than what they have been getting. When a person convinces themselves that they deserve to get what they want, this keeps them from seeing beyond themselves. Therefore, everything they do is designed around self-satisfaction. They become set up for continual wounding through disappointment, because of the feelings of rejection attached to not getting what you think you deserve.

The Cambridge Dictionary defines entitlement as, "Something that you have a right to do or have, or the right to do or have something; the feeling that you have the right to do or have what you want without having to work for it or deserve it, just because of who you are."[19]

This sense of entitlement will keep you stuck emotionally when you deeply feel that you didn't deserve what life has dished out to you. It also reflects on how you see God, if you feel that what you received was something He should have and/or could have prevented.

The book of Job gives a subtle example of how the spirit of entitlement can creep in, when a person is experiencing a time of trial and suffering. The things that were hidden in Job's heart were brought to the surface. He did everything he knew to do to make sure everything would go well with him and his household (Job 1:1-3). He was considered blameless and upright, a man of great status in the East. He would rise early in the morning to offer sacrifices up for his children after the days of feasting just in case they may have sinned against God in their hearts (Job 1:5).

The book of Job tells a story of a man who experienced unmerited (undeserved) suffering. We are often taught that all throughout the suffering, Job never lost faith in God. In *chapter 1 vs. 22* we read, *"In all this Job did not sin nor charge God with wrong."*

There are things embedded deep within our hearts that we may not be consciously aware of, and God will cause those things to rise to the surface when we experience emotional woundedness throughout our Christian journey. God doesn't just accept what comes out of our mouth; He is more interested in what is in our hearts. *"For the Lord does not see as man sees; for man looks at the outward appearance, but the Lord looks at the heart," (I Samuel 16:7b).* The feeling of entitlement is an attitude of the heart which, when unchecked, will cause us to err in our judgment and behavior.

In the first chapter of Job, *verse 21* after the loss of his family and substance, Job declared, *"Naked I came from my mother's*

---

[19] https//disctionary.cambridge.org

womb, and naked shall I return there. The Lord gave, and the Lord has taken away. Blessed be the name of the Lord." However, in *chapter 3 verses 1-2*, after he was afflicted in his body, he had this to say: *"After this Job opened his mouth and cursed the day of his birth. And Job spoke and said: May the day perish in which I was born, and the night in which it was said, 'A male child is conceived.'"* Job did not curse God directly but cursing the day he was born was a display of anger that is indirectly targeted towards the one who made the decision for him to be born. Despising the day he was born indicates a focus on what he was dealing with in the present that seems undeserving and unfair.

When the feeling of entitlement is in our hearts because of loss, disappointment, or other unpleasant experiences we are having, or have had, we can unknowingly hold onto anger, resentment, bitterness, and unforgiveness toward God. This may sound very strong to some because religion will tell us it's being irreverent to be angry, disappointed, or even question God when we don't feel our expectations have been met. This is a deception of our hearts that projects a false sense of security, which hides our true feelings, thus hindering our growth. There is an invisible wall erected between us and God, which makes it very difficult to go to Him for healing when deep in our hearts we are angry or disappointed with Him. How many of us feel comfortable in approaching someone we are angry with for help? It becomes very difficult to go before God, because where there is anger, hurt, disappointment, etc., there will be a lack of trust.

It is in our human nature to question what we don't understand or agree with. The ability to be transparent with God determines whether we are

The ability to be transparent with God determines whether we are serving Him out of religion or out of relationship.

serving Him out of religion or out of relationship. Religion will cause us to build walls around our hearts because we are relating to Him through works (our gifts, talents, and abilities). God sent His son, Jesus, so we could have relationship with Him that is based on trusting His love for us and allows for intimacy—in-to-me-see—with Him. *Psalms 51:6 tells us, "Behold, You desire truth in the inward parts, And in the hidden part You will make me to know wisdom."*

I strongly believe God is not intimidated by our anger, disappointments, or questions, since He already knows what is in our hearts before we do. Most of the time, we don't know what's in our hearts until the sufferings, trials, conflicts, loss, and disappointments we experience reveal them to us.

God did not respond to Job's dialog with a defense but with one of many questions in Job chapter 38. This spoke to where Job was located and was used to reset him: *"Then the Lord answered Job out of the whirlwind, and said: 'Who is this who darkens counsel by words without knowledge? Now prepare yourself like a man; I will question you, and you shall answer me,'" (Job 38:1-3).*

When God asks us a question, it is not because He's looking for answers; He is Omniscient, all knowing. He asks us a question to get our attention, direct our focus so we can see and hear what is hidden in our hearts. *God speaks to the root of the matter and not the fruit displayed.* I have experienced times when God has asked me questions about something that revealed an issue of my heart that I was totally unaware of. I confidently knew it was God speaking to me by His Holy Spirit, because my attention was far from the subject, so the unexpected question bypassed my mind and went directly to my heart.

When God asked the question in *chapter 38:4, "Where were you*

When God asks us a question, it is not because He's looking for answers;

when I laid the foundations of the earth? Tell me if you have understanding." I believe He was speaking to Job's sense of entitlement that was hidden in his heart.

God speaks to the root of the matter and not the fruit displayed.

God didn't ask Job anything about the suffering he was currently experiencing, but He spoke to what Job had spoken of in *Job chapter 3:25*, a root of entitlement based on fear: *"For the thing I greatly feared has come upon me, and what I dreaded has happened to me."*

Fear is one of the main weapons the enemy uses to turn our attention on ourselves, because we feel that something or someone will hinder, threaten, or cause us pain. We will harbor this sort of fear because we feel we are entitled to that which the fear is attached to. Job did everything right that he knew to do and was commended for it by God in His dialog with Satan in Job chapters 1 and 2. God wants what we do for Him to be out of love and not fear. When what we do is out of love, there will not be emotional strings of entitlement attached; we are doing it unto the Lord, and not to receive a reward we feel we deserve from our efforts.

"Where were you when I laid the foundations of the earth? Tell me if you have understanding."

It is very important that the hidden feelings of entitlement be revealed to us because if it is hidden, the enemy will use it to build a spiritual wall between us and God. Once it has been revealed to us, then God is able, through the Spirit of Truth, to help us understand and embrace God's sovereignty and His divine justice. In an essay by John M. Frame, he states: [20]

---

[20] https://www.thegospelcoalition.org 2021

> The sovereignty of God is the fact that He is the Lord over creation; as sovereign, He exercise His rule. This rule is exercised through God's authority as king, His control over all things, and His presence with His covenantal people and throughout His creation.

The sovereignty of God basically means that God is the ultimate source of all power and authority, and has the final decision in all things as any ruler would have. This calls for our submission and can bring us peace and comfort knowing He is in control. When we understand and embrace God's sovereignty in all things, it will help to cancel those feelings of entitlement that tell us we deserve better, which can lead to mental and emotional torment. Accepting God's sovereignty concerning a matter will also shut the voices of blame, unworthiness, and condemnation that may come through the voice of friends like Job's, our own human voice, or the voice of the enemy. These voices will tell us that we don't deserve what happened to us. They may try to tell us that God is unfair, or that it was somehow our fault that we should have or could have done something different to cause a different outcome.

We find in chapter 1 that Job had done the right thing, yet he experienced tremendous loss and suffering. He is a prime example of the fact that bad things do happen to good people. How many of us can testify with brother Job that we didn't sign up for that part of our Christian journey? Perhaps you may have been blindsided by some unexpected emotional trauma that you haven't been able to resolve. The Word of God within us, which generates our faith, will be tried, and tested in all of us!

Job chapter 2 shows us that the integrity and uprightness of Job, which never faltered, was being challenged by Satan. The test did show, however, that amid his suffering, Job asked the question "why" (for what reason, can you explain to me?). The "why" question is sometimes asked, because we don't understand the reason things happened the way they did, especially when we were expecting a better result. Job needed to know, as we all do at times, that even though everything humanly possible was done to move a situation in another direction, we find out that doing the right thing will not always guarantee the outcome we feel we have the right to. There will be times when God will answer our "why" questions and sometimes not. One of the questions I ask a person who is stuck with the "why" question is, "How will knowing why help you?" What I have found at times is there's an element of control involved that is also rooted in fear. They feel that knowing why would become a defense mechanism to use to keep it from happening again. Sometimes the answer to the "why" question is maybe because God said so!

The Word of God within us, which generates our faith, will be tried, and tested in all of us!

Job's wife didn't understand how he could still maintain his integrity towards God when all the tragic events happened and suggested that he *"curse God and die." (Job 2:9b)*. This is where the sovereignty of God will supersede our thoughts and expectations and will help us to accept it to move on. *"But he said to her, 'You speak as one of the foolish women speaks. Shall we indeed accept good from God, and shall we not accept adversity?' In all this Job did not sin with his lips," (Job 2:10)*. The more I walk with God, the more I expect the unexpected!

Selah Moment: "*And the Lord turned the captivity of Job, when he prayed for his friends: also, the Lord gave Job twice as much as he had before*" *(Job: 42:10)*. Job's captivity was turned around when he prayed instead of judging his friends for their treatment towards him, while he was being challenged. Praying for others who have wounded you will cause your focus to go beyond yourself. Job had to go beyond himself to experience breakthrough. When we take the focus off ourselves, the situation, and the effects of the situation on us through prayer, there is a releasing that takes place within our soul (mind, will, and emotions). The error of entitlement will no longer reside in our hearts and will allow emotional healing to begin.

Take this time and allow Holy Spirit to show you those disappointing times when your expectations were met with feelings of confusion, disappointment, unfairness, or undeserved treatment. Begin to offer prayers of forgiveness, releasing everyone involved: yourself, others, God, and the attached painful emotions.

_____

_____

_____

_____

_____

_____

_____

"For my thoughts are not nothing like your thoughts," says the Lord. "And my ways are far beyond anything you could imagine."
Isaiah 55:8, NLT

Chapter 9
The Pit of Pride

Pride is a human paradox, where what is displayed on the outside is the opposite of what is on the inside. It is a projection of the vulnerabilities that lie within a person. Pride is a defense mechanism that proves true the Scripture found in *Proverbs 16:18: "Pride goes before destruction, and a haughty spirit before a fall."* It sets us up for failure, because of the deception that lurks behind it. There is a lack of truth towards others, God, and self. Pride forms a pit around us. That pit surrounds us on all sides with walls, and these walls keep others out, but also keep us confined and hardens our hearts. The walls of pride can be slippery and hard to climb to become free. The walls are also high enough to not allow the light of God's truth to enter in.

Pride is also a deflection for insecurity, unworthiness, shame, low self-esteem, rejection, self-rejection, self-hatred, inadequacy, feelings of failure, abandonment, and various forms of abuse.

Is There Any Meat on the Bones?

Pride is a form of denial that blankets the hidden things of the heart.

When a person must "toot their own horn," it's usually because deep down inside there is a fear that no one else will. We learn in doing spiritual warfare to discern what is below the surface, because that is where the roots are. Pride is a form of denial that blankets the hidden things of the heart.

Just as pride reflects the opposite of what we have hidden inside it has the opposite effect on those around us. It generates more hurt because of its repelling nature. This shows the power of deception; we think it will cause us to be more acceptable, but to those who are exposed to our pride, it causes a repulsion to take place. Pride is a sinful self-protector, because the person is using their flesh instead of the Holy Spirit as protection from the possibility of being wounded by rejection, abandonment, etc.

We read in *John 10:10a, "The thief does not come except to steal, and to kill, and to destroy."* The enemy of our souls uses pride as one of his weapons of mass destruction to sabotage the life of the believer in Christ. The following excerpt gives a good illustration of how the thief uses pride to cheat us out of so many things pertaining to the Kingdom of God.

My Name is Pride by Beth Moore[21]

- My name is Pride. I am a cheater.
- I cheat you of your God-given destiny…because you demand your own way.
- I cheat you of contentment…because you "deserve better than this."
- I cheat you of knowledge…because you already know it all.

---

[21] *Praying God's Word-Breaking Free From Spiritual Strongholds*; B & H Books, September 1, 2009, pgs. 59 & 60.

- I cheat you of healing...because you're too full of me to forgive.
- I cheat you of holiness...because you refuse to admit when you're wrong.
- I cheat you of vision...because you'd rather look in the mirror than out a window.
- I cheat you of a genuine friendship...because nobody's going to know the real you.
- I cheat you of love...because real romance demands sacrifice.
- I cheat you of greatness in heaven...because you refuse to wash another's feet on earth.
- I cheat you of God's glory...because I convince you to seek your own.
- My name is Pride. I am a cheater.
- You like me because you think I'm always looking out for you. Untrue.
- I'm looking to make a fool of you.
- God has so much for you, I admit, but don't worry...
- If you stick with me-you'll never know.

The good news is that Jesus Christ was sent to the earth to be an example for us to follow, so that we can navigate through relational challenges where pride would try to dominate. Let's look at one of the primary examples He displayed for us and some principles:

> "Let this mind be in you which was also in Christ Jesus, who, being in the form of God, did not consider it robbery to be equal with God, but

made Himself of no reputation, taking the form of a bondservant, and coming in the likeness of men. And being found in appearance as a man, He humbled Himself and became obedient to the point of death, even the death of the cross."
Philippians 2:5-8

1. *Vs. 5:* Allowing our minds (part of our soul) to be in alignment with the mind of Christ. Instead of the phrase W.W.J.D. (What Would Jesus Do?), we want to focus on *what did Jesus do?* The example He set and the words He spoke, indicated where His mind was. Jesus said to His disciples, *"For I have come down from Heaven, not to do My own will, but the will of Him who sent Me," (John 6:38).* This should be our motivation, that all we do is done unto the Lord.

2. *Vs. 6: Being confident of who we are because of whose we are.* This confidence in God causes us to believe what He says about us above what anyone else may say about us. Jesus was so confident in who He was that He didn't have to contend with His Father for position, because He was one with the Father. When we are confident in who we are, there will be no need to promote ourselves or compete with others. There will be no fear of being robbed of the position or status we think we might hold.

3. *Vs. 7: We must empty ourselves of our own opinion of ourselves, to have a heart of a servant.* Jesus emptied Himself of His deity to come in human form to fulfill His assignment for the redemption of mankind. *"For what the law could not do in that it was weak through the flesh, God did by sending His own Son in the likeness of sinful flesh, on account of sin: He condemned sin in the flesh," (Romans 8:3).* Sometimes it takes humbling ourselves in

situations that will allow us to see God's purpose and plan for the future. A good temperature check as to whether you have a servant's heart is how you respond when you are treated like one!

> *A good temperature check as to whether you have a servant's heart is how you respond when you are treated like one!*

4. *Vs. 8:* Humbleness will cause death to the false sense of importance that empowers the spirit of pride. To be humble is to be "marked by meekness or modesty in behavior, attitude, or spirit, not arrogant or prideful".[22] The quality of being humble is called humility. Walking in humility is what we need to do, but like everything else, we need Holy Spirit to empower us to do it.

> "But the fruit of the [Holy] Spirit [the work of which His presence within accomplishes] is love, joy (gladness), peace, patience (an even temper, forbearance), kindness, goodness(benevolence), faithfulness, Gentleness (meekness, humility), self-control (self-restraint, continence). Against such things there is no law [that can be charged]. And those who belong to Christ Jesus (the Messiah) have crucified the flesh (the godless human nature) with its passions and appetites and desires. If we live by the [Holy] Spirit, let us also walk by the Spirit. [If by the Holy Spirit we have our life in God, let us go forward walking in line, our conduct controlled by the Spirit."
> Galatians 5:22-25, AMPC

---

[22] https://www.yourdictionary.com

There are many ways that walking in humility will benefit us. We are exhorted in the scriptures that humility should be worn as a garment. It becomes a protective covering to shield us from the pit of pride.

> "Therefore, as the elect of God, holy and beloved, put on tender mercies, kindness, humility, meekness, longsuffering."
> Colossians 3:12

> "Likewise, you younger people, submit yourselves to your elders. Yes, all of you be submissive to one another, and to be clothed with humility, for 'God resists the proud, But gives grace to the humble."
> I Peter 5:5

We can see from these scriptures that humility requires action on our part to put it on, which allows us to walk in it. *"He has shown you, O man, what is good; And what does the Lord require of you But to do justly, To love mercy, And to walk humbly with your God?" (Micah 6:8)*. It took humbling to receive salvation. Humbly confessing that we were sinners in need of a Savior was only the beginning of our walk in humility, and humility must remain a part of our lives until eternity calls us home.

Let's look at some other benefits of humility that outweighs anything that the spirit of pride might want to offer us:

- "But He gives more grace. Therefore, He says: 'God resist the proud, But gives grace to the humble." James 4:6
- "Therefore, humble yourself under the mighty hand of God, that He may exalt you in due season." I Peter 5:6
- "... He does not forget the cry of the humble." Psalms 9:12b

- "Lord, You have heard the desire of the humble;" Psalms 10:17b
- "The humble He guides in justice, And the humble He teaches His way." Psalms 25:9
- "The Lord lifts up the humble; He casts the wicked down to the ground." Psalms 147:6
- "For the Lord takes pleasure in His people; He will beautify the humble with salvation." Ps. 149:4
- "By humility and the fear of the Lord Are riches and honor and life." Proverbs 22:4
- "A man's pride will bring him low, But the humble in spirit will retain honor." Proverbs 29:23
- ". . . I dwell in the high and holy place, with him who has a contrite and humble spirit, To revive the spirit of the humble, And to revive the heart of the contrite ones." Isaiah 57:15b

Pride involves self-exaltation and is a primary tool used by the enemy, who lost his place in glory for the same reason (Isaiah 14:13). Pride blocks our view in so many areas, which robs us of the opportunity to grow in the grace of God. It keeps us from learning, forgiving, and walking in unity with one another.

> "Since God chose you to be the holy people He loves, you must clothe yourselves with tenderhearted mercy, kindness, humility, gentleness, and patience. Make allowance for each other's faults, and forgive anyone who offends you. Remember, the Lord forgave you, so you must forgive others."
> Colossians 3:12-13

Selah Moment: *"For I say, through the grace given to me, to everyone who is among you, not to think of himself more highly than he ought to think, but to think soberly, as God has dealt to each one a measure of faith," (Romans 12:3).* Healthy self-esteem is when we think soberly of ourselves; that we are who we are because of who God is in us. We receive the blessing of God's grace to accomplish everything in our lives, and God gets the glory! Walking in humility requires faith in God's word and His love for us so as not to allow pride to operate within us as a sinful self-protector.

Do you sometimes feel attacked and the need to defend yourself when you receive any criticism towards you or your abilities? Ask Holy spirit to show you if pride is in operation, list below those things Holy Spirit reveals to you, repent, and allow Him to continue to grace you with humility for future situations.

Walking in humility requires faith in God's word and His love for us so as not to allow pride to operate within us as a sinful self-protector.

_____

_____

_____

_____

_____

_____

"Let another man praise you, and not your own mouth;
A stranger, and not your own lips."
Proverbs 27:2

Part 4
How Is The Meat Separated?

Our part in separating the meat from the bones is following the example of Jesus and utilizing the tools given to us as blood-washed, spirit-filled Christians. Oftentimes, we will encounter spiritual battles for our soul or spiritual warfare. In the midst of the battle, the enemy will continually attempt to blind us to what God wants us to see. We are given the responsibility to have an open heart and allow Holy Spirit, the Spirit of Truth, to search our hearts to make sure there's no "wicked ways" in us (see Psalms 139:23-24). We can't fight the powers without until we gain victory over the powers within. Jesus prayed for Peter because He knew the future challenges that awaited him:

> *We can't fight the powers without until we gain victory over the powers within.*

> "And the Lord said, 'Simon, Simon! Indeed, Satan has asked for you, that he may sift you as wheat. But I have prayed for you, that your faith should not fail; and when you have returned to Me, strengthen your brethren."
> Luke 22:31-32

"Be anxious for nothing, but in everything by
prayer and supplication, with thanksgiving, let your
requests be made known to God."
Philippians 4:6

Prayer holds the keys to the Kingdom of God that causes Heaven to touch earth during our personal challenges. Prayer will direct our focus to what heaven's view is about our situation. When we pray the prayer that Jesus taught His disciples, we are also inviting God's will for our situation to reflect heaven here on earth:

What you digest will either strengthen you or weaken you.

"So He said to them, 'When you pray, say: Our
Father in heaven, Hallowed be Your name. Your
Kingdom come. Your will be done
On earth as it is in heaven."
Luke 11:2

Sometimes separating the meat from the bones involves separating ourselves from people who negatively feed the wounded side of us. When we fellowship with people who constantly murmur and complain about things in the church, it will negatively influence us. Protect your ear gate from what you hear as it may fuel your woundedness and hinder your ability to receive insight and healing. What you digest will either strengthen you or weaken you. In his book, *The Eagle Christian*, Kenneth Price writes about how the eagle behaves in sickness.[23] The eagle maintains a specific diet of fresh meat.

---

[23] Price, Kenneth, The Eagle Christian, Old Faithful Press, Wetumka, Alabama, 1984, p. 46.

However, there are times when he will digest meat that is diseased and becomes sick. The following is an excerpt from chapter 13 of that book:

> However, it is possible for an eagle to devour some creature, and get food poisoning. When this happens, the eagle becomes weak. Although this is a serious problem, it does not usually result in the death of an eagle. The eagle instincts take over and he will locate some inaccessible place, such as a cliff or butte, and lie prostate in the sunlight with his wing spread wide open. Once the eagle has done this, he will fix his eyes firmly on the sun until the warmth of the sun and his natural body processes have returned his strength.
>
> From chapter three, we discovered that the eagle's source of strength is his diet, and the same is true of the Eagle Christian. It is quite possible that some untruth, which looks good and smells good and certainly tastes good, could get into the diet of the Eagle Christian. When this happens, he/she becomes ill. At this point, he/she must allow their spiritual instincts to take over and prostrate themselves before God, letting His light of truth and the warmth of love do healing work, as the Eagle Christian stares unchangingly at the Son. Like the eagle, this must be done in a place of solitude for the work to be safe and complete.

The illustration of the eagle gives us another good reason why prayer is so important in helping us separate the meat from the bones. We look to Jesus, who is the one that made provision for our healing when our faith has been weakened by life's challenges.

> "Looking unto Jesus, the author and finisher of our faith, who for the joy that was set before Him endured the cross, despising the shame, and has sat down at the right hand of the throne of God."
> Hebrews 12:2

> "For there is one God and one Mediator between God and man, the Man Christ Jesus."
> I Timothy 2:5

> "Seeing that we have a great High Priest who has passed through the heavens, Jesus the Son of God, let us hold fast our confession. For we do not have a High Priest who cannot sympathize with our weaknesses, but was in all points tempted as we are, yet without sin. Let us therefore come boldly to the throne of grace, that we may obtain mercy and find grace to help in time of need."
> Hebrews 4:14-16

Praise and worship are also tools we can use to help us separate the meat from the bones. Praise and worship shift our focus off the problem and places it on the Problem Solver. Praise is adoration towards God and the giving of thanks for the things He has and continues to give us, such as His lovingkindness, His goodness, His mercy, His protection, His faithfulness, etc. When we praise God, we are reminded of what He has previously done for us; if He's done it before, He will do it again!

"Enter into His gates with thanksgiving, And into His courts with praise. Be thankful to Him, and bless His name."
Palms 100:4

Praise and worship shift our focus off the problem and places it on the Problem Solver.

"Oh, give thanks to the Lord! Call upon His name; Make known His deeds among the peoples!"
I Chronicles 16:8

"But you are a chosen generation, a royal priesthood, a holy nation, His own special people, that you may proclaim the praises of Him who called you out of darkness into His marvelous light."
I Peter 2:9

Worship goes deeper than praise, and is more intimate, because we are acknowledging God for *who* He is. Our focus is not only removed from our concerns, but we have entered that most holy place where God is able to bring healing. This is the place in the temple of the Old Testament, the Holy of Holies, located behind the veil, where the sacrifices were made by the High Priest and God came down as a consuming fire to receive it. During this time of intimacy with God, we are presenting ourselves before Him as a living sacrifice. He ministers to us and exchanges the ashes of our emotional pain for His beauty (see Isaiah 61:3b).

"I beseech you therefore, brethren, by the mercies of God, that you present your bodies a living sacrifice, holy, acceptable to God, which is your reasonable service."
Romans 12:1

> "Oh come, let us worship and bow down; Let us kneel before the Lord our Maker For He is our God, And we are the people of His pasture and the sheep of His hand. Today, if you will hear His voice."
> Psalms 95:6-7

> "Give to the Lord the glory due to His name; Worship the Lord in the beauty of holiness."
> Psalms 29:2

> "For our God is a consuming fire."
> Hebrews 12:29

The Power of Forgiveness

A very important tool that is a necessary requirement in our quest to separate the meat from the bones is our willingness to forgive. Forgiveness is very instrumental in igniting the healing process. The need to forgive can involve ourselves and God, as well as others that we feel have hurt us or someone we love. Forgiveness is not a feeling but an act of our will in obedience to the Word of God.

> "Bearing with one another, and forgiving one another, if anyone has a complaint against another; even as Christ forgave you, so you also must do."
> Colossians 3:13

> "For if you forgive men their trespasses, your heavenly Father will also forgive you. But if you do not forgive men their trespasses, neither will your Father forgive your trespasses."
> Matthew 6:14-15

Choosing to forgive those who have hurt us will not only release them, but we also release ourselves. To hold someone captive with unforgiveness, we must stand guard over our hearts, resulting in self-imprisonment. Forgiveness does not make the injury we received leave immediately, because forgiving doesn't mean you forget. Forgiveness is giving up your right to be right and trusting God to heal the wound caused by the injury.

> "Therefore I always exercise and discipline myself [mortifying my body, deadening my carnal affections, bodily appetites, and worldly desires, endeavoring in all respects] to have a clear (unshaken, blameless) conscience void of offense toward God and toward man."
> Acts 24:16, AMPC

Forgiveness is giving up your right to be right and trusting God to heal the wound caused by the injury.

The following is a summary of a few benefits obtained by operating in forgiveness taken from the book, *Forgiving What You'll Never Forget*.[24]

Physical Benefits: "There are apparently two ways that forgiveness benefits us physically. One way is through the reduction of stress. These negative emotions will increase our

---

[24] Stoop, Dr. David, *Forgiving What You'll Never Forget*, Revell a division of Baker Publishing Group, Grand Rapids, MI 2001, 2003, pgs. 143-149.

blood pressure and lead to hormonal changes that are linked to heart disease, the impairment of our immune system, and even to impaired neurological functions, including our memory. The second way forgiveness benefits us physically is that forgiving people have stronger social networks. People with stronger friendships and strong familial networks and social networks are healthier."

> *Forgiveness restores the belief that we have some power over what happens in our own lives."*

Emotional Benefits: "We often believe we are retaining or regaining a sense of power and control when we withhold forgiveness, but that is a false sense of control. We think we are in control, but the truth is quite the opposite. When we forgive, we actually regain self-control when we give up control. Forgiveness restores the belief that we have some power over what happens in our own lives."

Relational Benefits: "Perhaps one of the greatest benefits we can experience when we forgive is the possibility of a restored relationship. Forgiveness is an essential ingredient for a successful, satisfying marriage and happy, successful families. In families where forgiveness is taught by both word and example, negative outcomes are minimized."

Spiritual Benefits: "When we give up our unforgiving spirit, we experience new freedom in our personal lives and new meaning in our spiritual lives. We don't feel as isolated. We are more at peace with our faith and beliefs. We feel like God is there, present in our lives, and we have a wider perspective on all of life that adds meaning to our own lives."

Once we are obedient to the responsibility God has given us, then we will be on our way to seeing clearly. The following Scripture is one of the first steps in Spiritual Warfare that is universal for all Christians, in order to experience victory in whatever conflict we may find ourselves in:

> "Being in a readiness to punish every [insubordinate for his disobedience, when your own submission and obedience [as a church] are fully secured and complete."
> II Corinthians 10:6, AMPC

There was a phrase that appeared to be coined at the beginning of the 19th century as the three basic skills to be taught in schools named the three "Rs.": reading, writing, and arithmetic, (usually said as "reading, writing, and 'rithmetic").[25] There are also three "Rs" that serve as the basic ingredients in the life of a Christian: repentance, renunciation, and rededication.

Repentance: The biblical definition of repentance is to make a change of mind, heart, and action by turning away from sin and self and returning to God.[26] Altar calls for repentance outside of the call to salvation are becoming exercised less and less in churches today. Repentance is an important instrument in our Christian walk to separate us from those hurts that would try to attach themselves to us. Repentance wipes our slate clean of negative situations, refocuses and renews us, bringing a refreshing.

---

[25] https://en.m.wikipedia.org
[26] https://www.learnreligions.com, Zavada, Jack, 2020

> "Now repent of your sins and turn to God, so
> that your sins may be wiped away, then times of
> refreshment will come from the presence of the Lord."
> Acts 3:19, NLT

Renunciation: The formal rejection of something, typically a belief, claim or course of action.[27] When we renounce those things that try to interrupt our joy and peace of mind, a declaration of separation is being made that you are no longer identifying it as being a part of your emotional makeup. The biblical definition is to refuse to follow, obey, or recognize any further.[28] You are no longer renting out space to the enemy (giving him access) but you are walking in the authority you have been given.

> "We have renounced disgraceful ways (secret
> thoughts, feelings, desires and underhandedness, the
> methods, and arts that men hide through shame);
> we refuse to deal craftily (to practice trickery and
> cunning) or to adulterate or handle dishonestly the
> Word of God, but we state the truth openly (clearly
> and candidly). And so we commend ourselves
> in the sight and presence of God to every man's
> conscience."
> II Corinthians 4:2, AMPC

Rededication: The act of rededication means to humble yourself, confess your sin to the Lord, and return to God with all your heart, soul, mind, and being.[29] When something is dedicated, it

---

[27] https://www.lexico.com, 2022
[28] https://www.merriam-webster.com
[29] https://www.learnreligions.com

has been set apart for some purpose. We have been set apart for the purposes of God and we can lose sight of that purpose when we have been emotionally wounded. Rededication enables us to become refocused, return whole heartedly to God and continue on the path God had ordained for us from the beginning.

> "And be constantly renewed in the spirit of your mind [having a fresh mental and spiritual attitude], And put on the new nature (the regenerate self) created in God's image, [Godlike] in true righteousness and holiness."
> Ephesians 4:23-24, AMPC

Selah Moment: I was on my knees one day praying about a very serious, emotionally draining situation I had been dealing with for some time. During my prayer, Holy Spirit brought a scripture to me from the *2nd chapter of the book of Deuteronomy verse 3: "You have compassed this mountain long enough: turn you northward."* This was my confirmation that it was time for me to do what I needed to do according to the guidelines established in His word, to separate myself from that situation which had me wandering in an emotional wilderness and to turn my focus towards God. That one word from Holy spirit changed the course of my life forever. There are times when God will speak to our heart regarding a situation and our obedient response becomes the first step in experiencing emotional freedom.

List below those areas revealed to you that can assist you in separating the meat from the bones in your life.

_____

_____

_____

_____

_____

_____

_____

_____

"In conclusion, be strong in the Lord [be empowered through your union with Him]; draw your strength from Him [that strength which His boundless might provide]."
Ephesians 6:10, AMPC

Chapter 10
God's Surgical Scalpel

God has His own "surgical scalpel," which is the Word of God (see Hebrews 4:12), that can bring separation of those things that hinder us on our Christian journey. After we have allowed Holy Spirit to show us our responsibility and how we have been empowered to separate the "meat from the bones," our hearts become open and prepared to see and receive the truth of our situations that sets us free. God's most powerful instrument of separation is His Word.

> "All Scripture is inspired by God and is useful to teach us what is true and to make us realize what is wrong in our lives. It corrects us when we are wrong and teaches us to do what is right. God uses it to prepare and equip his people to do every good work."
> 2 Timothy 3:16-17, NLT

God's Word is able to bring truth to any circumstance because it was breathed by God's Spirit and therefore, directly relates to Him. "Truth is that which is consistent with the mind, will, character, glory, and being of God. Truth is the self-expression of God."[30] The scriptures testifies that God is truth:

> "Then Jesus said to those Jews who believed Him, 'If you abide in My word, you are My disciples indeed. And you shall know the truth, and the truth shall make you free."
> John 8:31-32

> "The entirety of Your word is truth, And every one of Your righteous judgments endures forever."
> Psalms 119:160

> "He is the Rock, His work is perfect; For all His ways are justice, A God of truth and without injustice; Righteous and upright is He."
> Deuteronomy 32:4

> "Jesus said to him. 'I am the way, the truth, and the life. No one comes to the Father except through Me."
> John 14:6

God is truth. Therefore, to know God is to know truth. God is the opposite of evil. The knowledge of His truth will help to abolish any evil belief that may be attempting to bring us trouble. When we read, study, and know His Word, it will help

---

[30] https://www.gty.org, *What is Truth*, John MacArthur, August 4, 2009

us to ultimately know His truth for our current situation. God's Word of truth is a powerful weapon to bring separation:

> "And take the helmet of salvation, and the sword of the Spirit, which is the word of God."
> Ephesians 6:17

> "For the Word that God speaks is alive and full of power [making it active, operative, energizing, and effective]; it is sharper than any two-edged sword, penetrating to the dividing line of the breath of life (soul) and [the immortal] spirit, and of joints and marrow [of the deepest parts of our nature], exposing and sifting and analyzing and judging the very thoughts and purposes of the heart."
> Hebrews 4:12, AMPC

God's sword of truth is a type of surgical scalpel that He uses in our lives. The surgeon uses his scalpel to cut out the diseased tissue, so the healing can begin. The same can occur in the spiritual realm as God's Word works an area of our life that needs attention to bring His truth and healing.

> "Now see that I, even I, am He, And there is no God besides Me; I kill and I make alive; I wound and I heal; Nor is there any who can deliver from My hand."
> Deuteronomy 32:39

> "For He bruises, but He binds up; He wounds, but His hands make whole."
> Job 5:18

> "Come, and let us return to the LORD; For He has torn, but He will heal us; He has stricken, but He will bind us up."
> Hosea 6:1

The life in God's Word brings healing and wholeness to whatever concerns us when we apply it.

God's Word promises to bring results in our lives because it is alive as we read in Hebrews 4:12. The life in God's Word brings healing and wholeness to whatever concerns us when we apply it. The following is a list of a few of the many attributes of God's Word to reassure and aid us in separating the meat from the bones in our lives:

It's everlasting:

> "But the word of the LORD endures forever." Now this is the word which by the gospel was preached to you."
> 1 Peter 1:25

> "Heaven and earth will pass away, but My words will by no means pass away."
> Matthew 24:35

> "The grass withers, the flower fades, But the word of our God stands forever."
> Isaiah 40:8

It travels:

> "He sends forth His word and heals them and rescues them from the pit and destruction."
> Psalms 107:20, AMPC

"But the officer said, "Lord, I am not worthy to have you come into my home. Just say the word from where you are, and my servant will be healed."
Matthew 8:8, NLT

It will not return empty:

"It is the same with my word. I send it out, and it always produces fruit. It will accomplish all I want it to, and it will prosper everywhere I send it."
Isaiah 55:11, NLT

"God is not a man, so he does not lie. He is not human, so he does not change his mind. Has he ever spoken and failed to act? Has he ever promised and not carried it through?"
Numbers 23:19, NLT

Judges the wicked:

"Fear of the LORD lengthens one's life, but the years of the wicked are cut short."
Proverbs 10:27, NLT

"The hope of the righteous will be gladness, But the expectation of the wicked will perish."
Proverbs 10:28

Do not fret because of evildoers, Nor be envious of the workers of iniquity. For they shall soon be cut down like the grass, And wither as the green herb."
Psalms 37:1-2

Perfects Love in us:

> "But whoever keeps His word, truly the love of God is perfected in him. By this we know that we are in Him."
> 1 John 2:5

> "But he who keeps (treasures) His Word [who bears in mind His precepts, who observes His message in its entirety], truly in him has the love of and for God been perfected (completed, reached maturity). By this we may perceive (know, recognize, and be sure) that we are in Him:"
> 1 John 2:5, AMPC

It shields and protects us:

> "Every word of God is tried and purified; He is a shield to those who trust and take refuge in Him."
> Proverbs 30:5, AMPC

> "God's way is perfect. All the LORD's promises prove true. He is a shield for all who look to him for protection."
> Psalms 18:30, NLT

Selah Moment: The Word of God is not only a powerful instrument to bring truth and healing in our lives, but it is also a preventative measure to back off satan as Jesus did when He was being tempted those three times in the wilderness. His response to the first of those temptations by Satan in *Matthew 4:4* set the patten of response for the other two: "*But He answered and said, 'It is written, Man shall not live by bread alone, but by every word that proceeds from the mouth of God.'*"

List below those scriptures that you can apply to areas of your life that are being challenged.

_____

_____

_____

_____

_____

_____

_____

_____

_____

_____

Is There Any Meat on the Bones?

_____

_____

_____

_____

_____

_____

_____

_____

_____

_____

_____

> Such things were written in the Scriptures long ago to teach us. And the Scriptures give us hope and encouragement as we wait patiently for God's promises to be fulfilled.
> Romans 15:4, NLT

Chapter 11
The Communion Table

The partaking of Holy Communion is practiced in some manner in the Christian community. It is a commemoration of the sacrifice of the body and blood of our Lord and Savior Jesus Christ, providing salvation to mankind. Yet it is another powerful weapon to enable us to see past our present pain to God's future promise.

Many Christians see Communion as a continuation of what is termed as the Last Supper. This is when Jesus sat down with His disciples just before His arrest and crucifixion. The scriptures tell us that His purpose for the meal was for celebrating the Feast of Passover (see Matthew 26, Mark 14, Luke 22, John 13). The celebration of Passover was first instituted in the Old Testament, located in the 12th chapter of the book of Exodus. The children of Israel were instructed by God through Moses on how to prepare and kill the Passover lamb so the blood could be applied to the doorpost of their homes. This was protection from the death angel which was sent to kill the first born in Egypt. This was done before they experienced their deliverance from the bondage of slavery they were experiencing in Egypt under Pharoah.

Jesus used the time during this special meal with His disciples to share with them the revelation of the unleavened bread and the blood of the lamb that was utilized during the Feast of Passover.

> "And as they were eating, Jesus took the bread, blessed, and broke it, and gave it to the disciples and said, 'Take, eat; this is My body." Then He took the cup, and gave thanks, and gave it to them, saying, 'Drink from it, all of you. For this is My blood of the new covenant, which is shed for many for the remission of sins."
> Matthew 26:26-28

> "Therefore purge out the old leaven, that you may be a new lump, since you truly are unleavened. For indeed Christ, our Passover, was sacrificed for us."
> I Corinthians 5:7

Jesus expressing the urgency in celebrating the Passover was not just in obedience to what His Father had commanded the Jewish nation to do every year, but because of what He was about to experience in the next few hours as the savior of the world.

> "When the hour had come, He sat down, and the twelve apostles with Him. Then He said to them, 'With fervent desire I have desired to eat this Passover with you before I suffer;"
> Luke 22:14-15

Jesus had knowledge of His future arrest, torture, and death, and knew He was sitting at a table with a betrayer, a denier, a doubter, and a bunch of deserters! Any one from this list would be enough for most of us to want to separate ourselves from, much less have a meal with! The potential for hurt can be experienced from either one of them when we have been in a close relationship with others as Jesus was with His disciples.

How much disappointment and emotional pain have we suffered when we find out, after the fact, the failures of others towards us? How violated we may feel because we trusted them and even made our heart vulnerable to them? Once we find out what was done to us, the last thing we would have a desire to do is to invite them to dinner. Jesus knew before the fact what the response towards Him would be after His arrest. He spoke of not just desiring to celebrate Passover with them, but as indicated in Luke 22:15, He had a *fervent* desire. A fervent person has or shows strong feelings about something and is very sincere and enthusiastic about it.[31] To desire means to long or hope for: conscious impulse toward something that promises enjoyment or satisfaction in its attainment.[32] How was Jesus able to rise above it all? He knew that reenacting the Passover would set an example for His disciples for theirs and our future challenges.

Jesus was able to not allow the present or His future to deter Him from what His assignment was on earth. The same thing will also apply to us as we explore the importance of celebrating the communion table at service and during our time of personal devotion. There is also the potential of continual revelation regarding the use of commemorating the body and blood of

---

[31] https://www.collinsdictionary.com 2022
[32] https://www.merriam-webster.com 2022

our Lord Jesus Christ to aid us in spiritual warfare. Therefore, Communion is always served when we have our Inner Healing and Deliverance Seminars.

Our faith can be activated as we take Communion, and we may find that deliverance will take place as partaking of communion is connected to the deliverance that took place during the celebration of the first Passover. Communion is all about Jesus and God's miraculous provision for us. In addition to deliverance, we can experience divine protection from the darts of the enemy with the appropriation of the blood of Jesus over our lives and the door post of our heart. We can also encounter healing of body, soul and spirit because of the stripes Jesus bore on our behalf on the cross of Calvary.

Partaking of communion is connected to the deliverance that took place during the celebration of the first Passover.

> "Surely He has borne our griefs and carried our sorrows; Yet we esteemed Him stricken, Smitten by God, and afflicted. But He was wounded for our transgressions, He was bruised for our iniquities; The chastisement for our peace was upon Him, And by His stripes we are healed."
> Isaiah 53:4-5

Celebrating the Communion Table on a regular basis will separate us from our woundedness and will place our focus on the provision of escape already made for us through our Lord and Savior Jesus Christ. Religion will try to dictate that we should be satisfied in taking Communion once a month or even once a year in some churches. However, there is no stipulation in the Word on how often we can take Communion or how old we must be to receive it. The Apostle Paul reveals in the following passage the revelation he received concerning the communion table:

> "For I received from the Lord Himself that which I passed on to you [it was given to me personally], that the Lord Jesus on the night when He was treacherously delivered up and while His betrayal was in progress took bread, And when He had given thanks, He broke [it] and said, 'Take, eat, This is My body which is broken for you. Do this to call Me [affectionately] to remembrance.' Similarly when supper was ended, He took the cup also, saying, 'This cup is the new covenant [ratified and established] in my blood. Do this, as often as you drink [it], to call me [affectionately] to remembrance.' For every time you eat this bread and drink this cup, you are representing and signifying and proclaiming the fact of the Lord's death until He comes [again]".
> I Corinthians 11:23-26, AMPC

These verses tell us that Communion can be taken often, and in doing so you are continually announcing the provision made through the death of Jesus until He returns. This would be a beneficial family teaching tool for those who celebrate the Communion Table at home on a regular basis. Young children can take Communion because they are under the covering of their adult parent/guardian who would be the ones responsible for being able to examine and rightly discern the Lord's body (see I Corinthians 11:28-29).

Selah Moment: Partaking of the Communion Table prepares us by doing a work in our heart because our focus is on Jesus and not on ourselves. Our enemies are not so much people, but the spirits that tend to work through people against us. The enemies of hurt, anger, betrayal, abandonment, false accusations, fear, unbelief, doubt, rejection, shame, guilt, disappointment, etc., will want to sit at our table. The table has been prepared by Jesus to separate us from them and render them powerless against us.

What revelation concerning the Communion Table are you able to apply during the season you are in to aid you in separating the meat from the bones? List below.

_____

_____

_____

_____

_____

_____

> "You prepare a table before me in the
> presence of my enemies;
> You anoint my head with oil; My cup runs over."
> Psalms 23:5

Part 5
Children, Have You Any Meat?

> "So Jesus said to them, 'Boys (children), you do not have any meat (fish) do you?' [Have you caught anything to eat along with your bread?] They answered Him No."
> John 21:5, AMPC

In this passage of Scripture, I believe Jesus was not only speaking to His disciples about physical food, but also about the meat pertaining to the Kingdom of God. This is the spiritual meat spoken of by Jesus earlier in the scriptures regarding doing the will of the Father and accomplishing His purpose for being sent to mankind to bring redemption.

> "Jesus said to them, My food (nourishment) is to do the will (pleasure) of Him Who sent Me and to accomplish and completely finish His work."
> John 4:34, AMPC

> "For the Kingdom of God is not eating and
> drinking, but righteousness and peace and joy in the
> Holy Ghost."
> Romans 14:17

The enemy of our soul may not cause us to backslide, but if he can prevent us from fulfilling our purpose for the Kingdom of God, he will have accomplished much. God's meat for us is to allow His will to be executed through us. In verse 3 of John chapter 21, Peter decided to go fishing, his previous occupation before following Jesus. It may seem comforting for us to go back to the familiar when we encounter life's disappointments, but it may not always be fruitful. Peter had his idea of what Jesus should do as He didn't want Him to be crucified (see Matthew 16:22, Mark 8:33). Only the Lord knows what emotional pain Peter and the disciples were in with the absence of Jesus.

In the same verse 3, the other disciples present followed Peter. Jesus had previously instructed His disciples that their calling went beyond the natural, yet they chose to pick their nets up again.

It may seem comforting for us to go back to the familiar when we encounter life's disappointments, but it may not always be fruitful.

> "And as He walked by the Sea of Galilee, He saw
> Simon and Andrew his brother casting a net into
> the sea; for they were fishermen. Then Jesus said to
> them, 'Follow Me, and I will make you
> become fishers of men.'
> They immediately left their nets and followed Him."
> Mark 1:16-18

The latter part of John 21:3 informs us that they fished all night and caught nothing. Once again, we always want to remember that when the Lord asks a question, it's not because He's trying to get information: He is an all-knowing God and He already knows the answer. I believe He sometimes will ask us a question to get our attention and/or to get us to pause and think.

After the disciples acknowledged their present status, we find that Jesus gave them direction on where to find the fish in *verse 6: "And He said to them, 'Cast the net on the right side of the boat, and you will find some.' So they cast, and now they were not able to draw it in because of the multitude of fish."*

Jesus encouraged them to cast their net on the right side of the boat. This could be interpreted as being the right side as opposed to the wrong side. Either one denotes a change of focus along with a change of direction. When the disciples obeyed, they were able to see and gather the fish (meat).

In our lives, we can lose sight of God's initial calling for our lives when we are caught in the "net" of emotional turmoil. We can invite Jesus to come into view, and He is able to give us the direction we need to arrive back on course and see the "meat of the matter."

Fish can also be a spiritual representation of souls. That day, the disciples caught a multitude that was symbolic of the future harvest and reaffirmed their original calling. God will reaffirm His will for our lives resulting in us becoming refocused. To do that, we must be willing to let go of the lack of productivity we may be experiencing and cast our net on the right side. The harvest is waiting for us to cast our net again, despite what we are or have been experiencing emotionally.

The year of the writing of this book (2022) is a Shemitah Year, according to the Hebrew calendar (see Leviticus 25). The Lord instructed the children of Israel to sow their field for six years but in the seventh year, they should keep a sabbath to the Lord and allow the land to rest. This was a time of letting go and trusting God for provision during that year when they were unable to reap the harvest from the land. It was and is now prophetically a time of releasing, letting go, and trusting God. God addressed any fears with the people that may surface concerning this step of faith:

> "And if you say, 'What shall we eat in the seventh year, since we shall not sow nor gather in our produce?' Then I will command My blessing on you the sixth year, and it will bring forth produce enough for three years."
> Leviticus 25:20-21

God will also command His blessing upon us when we release to Him emotions such as anger, bitterness, unforgiveness, regret, guilt, etc. He will always bless our obedience. There are many reasons that can make it difficult at times to let go of the emotions that hold us captive, but God reassures us that when we let go, His blessings will be upon us. Letting go is an act of our will and not an emotional one. In doing so, we are saying, "I am trusting Him above all that I might be going through." Letting go means you are walking by faith and not by sight.

> "Cast your burdens on the Lord, And He shall sustain you, He shall never permit the righteous to be moved."
> Palms 55:22

> "Casting the whole of your care [all your anxieties, all your worries, all your concerns, once and for all]

> on Him, for He cares for you affectionately and
> cares about you watchfully."
> I Peter 5:7 AMPC

The fourth chapter of the book of Hebrews speaks about the rest God has provided for us, which is another reflection of our obedience towards Him. To enter into this rest will require diligence on our part to rise above our mind, will, and emotions.

I asked Holy Spirit one day, "What is the blockage that occurs in a person who knows the Word, yet they have a difficult time walking in victory?" He spoke to my heart: "Their will and their emotions." These two parts of our soul have the potential to rob us of our ability to walk by faith.

> "Therefore, since a promise remains of entering His
> rest, let us fear lest any of you seem to have come
> short of it. For indeed the gospel was preached to us
> as well as to them; but the word which they heard
> did not profit them, not being mixed with faith in
> those who heard it. For we who have believed do
> enter that rest, as He has said."
> Hebrews 4:1-3

The story of Leah is found in the book of Genesis. She was one of the wives of Jacob who experienced much rejection because she was not his first choice; her sister Rachel was the one Jacob loved. God saw Leah was unloved and opened her womb first to bear children (Genesis 29:31). She bore her first three sons for Jacob, believing they would turn his heart towards her. The naming of her fourth son, Judah—which means praise—showed that she had changed her focus, let go, and entered a time of rest.

"So Leah conceived and bore a son, and she called his name Reuben; for she said. 'The Lord has surely looked on my affliction. Now therefore, my husband will love me.' Then she conceived again and bore a son, and said, 'Because the Lord has heard that I am unloved, He has therefore given me this son also.' And she called his name Simeon. She conceived again and bore a son, and said, 'Now this time my husband will become attached to me, because I have borne him three sons.' Therefore his name was called Levi. And she conceived again and bore a son, and said, 'Now I will praise the Lord.' Therefore she called his name Judah. Then she stopped bearing."
Genesis 29:32-35

Selah Moment: God did not say He opened Leah's womb to get Jacob to love her. I believe He not only opened her womb because He saw that she was unloved but also because *He* loved her. Our emotions can sometimes have us striving for that which doesn't reflect the heart, mind, and will of God. We can become loyal to that which is not loyal to us and find ourselves bearing fruit that will cause more disappointment and hurt.

Allow Holy Spirit to show you and list below, those things you may be holding on to emotionally, physically, or mentally that hinder you from walking in God's will for you.

_____

_____

_____

_____

_____

_____

_____

"Come to Me, all you who labor and are heavy laden, and I will give you rest. Take My yoke upon you and learn of Me, for I am gentle and lowly in heart, and you will find rest for your souls."
Matthew 11:28-29

Chapter 12
What Are Protein Blockers?

Our physical bodies need protein, such as found in meat, to help build muscle, repair tissue, and fight infection. Having too much protein can cause waste to build up in your blood, and your kidneys may not be able to remove all the extra waste.[33] People experiencing chronic kidney disease will be given treatments used to block proteins because this build-up can cause nausea, loss of appetite, weakness, and taste changes. In the Journal of the American Society of Nephrology, author Garabed Eknoyan states: [34]

> In the books of the Bible that follow the Pentateuch, mostly in Jeremiah and Psalms, the human kidneys

---

[33] https://www.kidney.org
[34] Journal of the American Society of Nephrology, Garabed Eknoyan, December 2005

are cited figuratively as the site of temperament, emotions, prudence, vigor, and wisdom. In five instances, they are mentioned as the organs examined by God to judge an individual. They are cited either before or after but always in conjunction with the heart as mirrors of the psyche of the person examined. (e.g., see Jeremiah 17:10, Psalms 26:2).

Unhealed hurts can serve as spiritual protein blockers to the eyes of our heart to prevent us from seeing the meat of God's truth. Being able to see God's meat in our challenging situations, will build us, heal us, shield us, and eliminate the lies of the enemy. These hurts will try to build up within us to overtake and weaken our faith as well as our ability to be used by God to our fullest potential.

"Keep your heart with all diligence, For out of it spring the issues of life."
Proverbs 4:23

When I read Scripture, God has graced me on many occasions to see the prospect of Inner Healing and/or deliverance. This rings true for me in the sixth chapter of the book of Isaiah, as an example of circumstances that can block our view regarding God, ourselves, and others. The prophet Isaiah had already been prophesying and seeing visions in the first five chapters, so why is it that he just saw the Lord in chapter 6? Was his view being blocked by something or someone *before* he received the vision? (Inquiring minds would like to know!)

"In the year that King Uzziah died, [in a vision] I saw the Lord sitting upon a throne, high and lifted up, and the skirts of His train filled the

[most holy part of the] temple."
Isaiah 6:1, AMPC

Using this example of the Prophet Isaiah, I would like to explore some possible reasons for the above-mentioned delay. Hopefully, they will be helpful in exposing how the enemy can use the same strategies to block our vision:

- It was during the year of King Uzziah's death that became a turning point in the life of Isaiah and his calling as a prophet. The reference to this event may have been used for historical reasons to mark when Isaiah was called. Symbolically, I believe it can also signify that sometimes there are things in our life that can block our view that we need to allow to die and stay dead. Dead things have no life in them, no strength, no hope, and no future. If we give the ashes of those dead things to God, He promises to exchange them for His beauty (see Isaiah 61:3), which is God's divine exchange!

- Some commentaries believe that the Prophet Isaiah and King Uzziah were first cousins. Family loyalty can be a very strong bond. This sort of bond is known as a soul tie. A soul tie is a strong emotional, spiritual, or physical bond with another person. In Isaiah's case, if they were truly related, this would be a natural soul tie due to their blood relationship. The fact that Uzziah was king, could have caused a divided loyalty with his relationship with God and his ability to see God as vivid as he did in the vision he received. People encounter soul ties in their lives that bind them to the wrong people. These are referred to as ungodly soul ties, which are developed emotionally, spiritually, and sexually. Ungodly soul ties can be the root to excessive, unnatural, or what's known as "inordinate affection" towards someone. Ungodly soul ties, if not broken over a person, will block their vision and keep them from seeing the meat and receive the breakthrough afforded them when truth is revealed.

- As ruler, King Uzziah was in an elevated position, and was looked up to by his subjects with admiration, adulation, and even possible worship. The position of king demanded honor, reverence, loyalty, respect, and obedience. Perhaps Uzziah's position as king put such a burden on Isaiah that his vision to see God was blocked.

Man was created to worship, specifically God. There is always that pull by the enemy to have man worship the seen rather than the unseen. When a leader or any person has been placed in an elevated position in our hearts, they can unknowingly become a type of idol to us. "Any person or thing that consumes your thoughts, words, time, energy, or money other than God is an idol."[35] Some idols require sacrifices; whether it is your time, emotions, needs, calling in God, affections, etc. Idols can also cause us to sacrifice the future on the altar of the now! When a person has been esteemed higher than God in our lives, it divides our heart, weakens our capacity to see truth, and delays our ability to be healed. The hurt comes because placing a person above God sets us up for disappointment, hurt, rejection, etc., when that person falls off their throne as their human weaknesses surface.

A person can become critical and judgmental when seeing their faults which opens the door to the enemy.

---

[35] https://www.bayviewbiblechurch.org, 2019

The meat of the matter is that we are called to our leader's anointing and not their shortcomings.

- The Prophet Isaiah's message was not always a popular one. He spoke to the people about their sins and the coming judgment. The truth is never popular when it conflicts with the belief, ideas, and behavior of others. One of our basic emotional human needs is to feel loved and accepted. Sometimes that need will weigh heavy on a person, and the influence of others can tempt them to compromise their beliefs due to the fear of abandonment and/or rejection. Being the bearer of unwanted truth and standing firm in it, can place a person in a position to be ostracized and rejected. These feelings of being ostracized and rejected can end up with the person harboring resentment, unknowingly in their heart, while carrying out their assignment. This can be a heavy burden for a person to bear when they are not secure in who they are in God and what they have been called to do.

- The Prophet Isaiah's ability to see God in His lofty place on the throne allowed him to see himself, the condition he was in spiritually, and the spiritual condition of the people he was associated with. Because he saw the Lord, he was able to get a bird's-eye view. Seeing God on the throne humbled the prophet and postured him into a position to recognize his own deficiencies.

We must recognize our own contribution to any given situation before we are able to experience emotional breakthroughs. There could be times that the decisions we make have put us in an unwanted predicament. Every decision we make has consequences, but bad decisions will make us victims.

This can occur when we make a life changing decision without God, believing Him for a good outcome, and feel disappointed when it doesn't end the way we want or expect. Once again, when a person feels victimized, they will: 1. Look for someone to rescue them; 2. Look for someone to blame; and 3. Live in a fantasy world of denial.

Isaiah's confession of his sins paved the way for his sanctification and preparation for ministry by Holy Spirit, represented by the coals removed from the altar used to purge his sins.

Every decision we make has consequences, but bad decisions will make us victims.

> "So I said: 'Woe is me for I am undone! Because
> I am a man of unclean lips, And I dwell in the
> midst of a people of unclean lips; For my eyes have
> seen the King, The Lord of hosts.' Then one of the
> seraphim flew to me, having in his hand a live coal
> which he had taken with the tongs from the altar.
> 7 And he touched my mouth with it, and said:
> 'Behold, this has touched your lips; Your iniquity is
> taken away, And your sin purged.'"
> Isaiah 6:5-7

I further believe that the possible blockages of guilt, shame, false burden, false responsibility, feeling of unworthiness and inadequacy, etc., were all removed and Isaiah was able to not only walk in his calling but to embrace it.

> "Also I heard the voice of the Lord, saying: 'Whom
> shall I send, And who will go for Us?'
> Then I said, 'Here am I! Send me.'"
> Isaiah 6:8

Selah Moment: In the *17th chapter of Jeremiah*, we are forewarned that our heart has the capacity to lie to us. *"The heart is deceitful above all things, And desperately wicked; who can know it?" (verse 9)*. It is very healthy to think well of ourselves, but we can't be naïve to the fact that we may have blind spots blocking our ability to see the total truth of a situation, including any error on our part. Jeremiah continues in *verse 10: "But I, the Lord, search all hearts and examine secret motives. I give all people their due rewards, according to what their actions deserve" (NLT)*.

Take some time to ask Holy Spirit to open the eyes of your heart to anything that maybe blocking your view of yourself and list below.

_____

_____

_____

_____

_____

_____

_____

_____

"Search me [thoroughly], O God,
and know my heart! Try me
and know my thoughts! And see if there
is any wicked or hurtful way in me, and
lead me in the way everlasting."
Psalms 139:23-24, AMPC

Chapter 13
What the Enemy Meant for Evil

According to *Romans 8:28*, there is no waste in God's economy: *"For we know that all things work together for good to those who love God, to those who are the called according to His purpose."* God uses everything and is able to use the bones we encounter for our good.

Bones and connective tissues can be boiled into what is known as bone broth, which is consumed for its rich minerals, vitamins, amino acids, and essential fatty acids. Even though the bones themselves can't be digested, and can cause injury if swallowed, the liquid from them is particularly beneficial for the healing of the digestive system by reducing inflammation.

One of the reasons inflammation can invade our body is through the exposure to toxins. Likewise, we become inflamed in our souls spiritually when we experience the toxicity of our woundedness. These "bones" that we have collected through hurtful encounters can be used by God to bring healing to us as He did during the time of Moses when the children of Israel were in the wilderness.

The children of Israel had gotten into trouble once again when they spoke against God and Moses in Numbers chapter 21 verse 5. God's response to their sin was to send fiery serpents among the people which bit them and caused many of them to die (verse 6). After the people had repented, Moses brought the matter before God through prayer (verse 7). The following was God's response to remedy the situation:

> "Then the Lord said to Moses, 'Make a fiery serpent and set it on a pole; and it shall be that everyone who is bitten, when he looks at it, shall live.' So Moses made a bronze serpent, and put it on a pole; and so it was, if a serpent had bitten anyone, when he looked at the bronze serpent, he lived."
> Numbers 21:8-9

Hurting people will ultimately hurt people.

In this story, God used the very thing that wounded them to bring healing. The bronze pole used by Moses was a symbol of sin, judgment, and human nature. When bronze vessels are used for foods, it helps in alkalizing and purifying the food being eaten or cooked in it. The fiery serpent set on the pole not only symbolized the punishment rendered, but by their obedience in looking at it, the people were healed.

Much of the emotional woundedness we experience is due to human contact. Hurting people will ultimately hurt people. This is a frequent tactic of the enemy to cause us to avoid the possibility of being hurt by avoiding people. The enemy knows that there is power in agreement which can ultimately be used against him. This is his age-old strategy to divide and conquer.

> "Again, I say to you that if two of you agree on earth
> concerning anything that they ask,
> it will be done for them by My Father in heaven."
> Matthew 18:19

The principle that God used with the Israelites in Numbers chapter 21 is a template of how He can use the very same instrument that hurt us to heal us. He instructed the people to look at the serpent, which represented the enemy who gained legal access because of their murmuring and complaining, rooted in rebellion. It's difficult to face the source of our woundedness without trusting God's love for us and His willingness and ability to bring healing. God spoke to the people through Moses, and they obeyed out of their trust in God which had not been exhibited in their previous behavior.

Those who have experienced the healing power of God are able to bring healing to others.

Those who have experienced the healing power of God are able to bring healing to others. Allowing God's healing power to work in your life is not just for you. God will use your personal testimony of victory to touch the lives of others. Our ability to bring healing to one another is expressed in the TPT Bible:[36]

---
[36] The Passion Translation, copyright 2017, 2018, 2020 by Passion & Fire Ministries, Inc.

> "Confess and acknowledge how you have offended
> one another and then pray for one another to be
> instantly healed, for tremendous power is released
> through the passionate, heartfelt prayer
> of a godly believer."
> James 5:16

There are other examples in the scriptures where bones were used by God to fulfill His purpose. He used the sensation of fire in the bones of Jeremiah. This helped him to rise above the overwhelming feelings that hindered his desire to prophesy anymore. He had a very unpopular ministry of exposing the wickedness of the people at that time. He experienced much rejection, was whipped, and placed in stocks by Pashhur, the son of a priest and governor of the house of the Lord.

> "Then I said, 'I will not make mention of Him, Nor
> speak anymore in His name.' But His word was in
> my heart like a burning fire Shut up in my bones; I
> was weary of holding it back, and I could not."
> Jeremiah 20:9

The enemy may not get you to leave the church, but if He can keep you on the sidelines instead of the frontlines, there will be a missing link created in the Body of Christ. God wants us to see that even the bones we encounter which may appear to overwhelm us negatively, can be used for His glory and our good.

In the book of *Ezekiel chapter 37*, the prophet was taken up by the Spirit of the Lord and sat down amid a valley full of dry bones. You may have found yourself experiencing a season in the valley where all you see is the dryness of life or dry bones. God wants you to know that He is able to use it for your good. When you invite the presence of the Lord as Ezekiel did, you will encounter God's ability to bring life to that situation. *"And He said to me, 'Son of man, can these bones live?' So I answered, 'O Lord God, You know'" (verse 3)*. God desires to breathe life into *our* dry places.

> "Also He said to me. Prophesy to the breath, prophesy, son of man, and say to the breath, 'Thus says the Lord God: Come from the four winds, O breath and breathe on these slain, that they may live.'" So I prophesied as He commanded me, and breath came into them, and they lived, and stood upon their feet, an exceedingly great army."
> Ezekiel 37:9-10

God assembled an army out of those dry bones when life was spoken to them. One word from God can profoundly change your life!. We're all a part of God's great army. As we embrace the fact that God will use the bones in our lives meant for evil for our good and His glory, we will see beyond those bones and experience the breath of life springing from this assurance. Always be on the lookout to see what God is doing in your situation and know that He is always up to something on your behalf and that it will work together for your good.

Always be on the lookout to see what God is doing in your situation

"Unto the upright there arises light in the darkness;
He is gracious, and full of compassion,
and righteous."
Psalms 112:4

"The righteous person faces many troubles, but the
Lord comes to the rescue each time.
Psalms 4:19, NLT

"Even when I walk through the darkest valley, I will
not be afraid, for you are close beside me. Your rod
and your staff protect and comfort me."
Psalms 23:4, NLT

Selah Moment: Max Lucado refers to the following statement as an audacious promise in his book, *God Will Use This for Good*:[37] "You'll get through this. It won't be painless. It won't be quick. But God will use this mess for good. In the meantime, don't be foolish or naïve. But don't despair either. With God's help, you will get through it."

List those valley experiences you have gone through or are going through where you have felt helpless, hopeless, or trapped and ask Holy Spirit to show you God's comfort, peace, protection, and rescue plan.

_____

_____

_____

_____

_____

_____

_____

_____

_____

_____

---

[37] Lucado, Max, *God Will Use This for Good*, Nashville, Tennessee by Thomas Nelson, 2013, page 2.

Is There Any Meat on the Bones?

_____

_____

_____

_____

_____

_____

_____

_____

_____

_____

_____

"In His kindness God called you to share
in His eternal glory
by means of Christ Jesus. So after you have suffered
a little while, He will restore, support, and strengthen you,
and He will place you on a firm foundation."
I Peter 5:10, NLT

Chapter 14
Could the Enemy Have Any Fears Concerning You?

Have you ever thought that there could be anything the enemy may fear about you? Think about what effect it could have on our emotional challenges, when we are able to see beyond our fears to see the threat we are to the enemy of our soul. This is especially true when we choose to focus on the meat (God's will and purpose) and not the bones, (the negative emotions felt). This thought came to me as I heard the following poem by Marianne Williamson many years ago being recited as an answer from one of the students who was asked by his coach, "What are your deepest fears?" in a scene from the movie, *Coach Carter*.[38]

---

[38] *Coach Carter*, Hollywood, CA., Paramount Pictures, 2005 APA

Is There Any Meat on the Bones?

"Our Deepest Fear"[39]

Our deepest fear is not that we are inadequate.
Our deepest fear is that we are powerful beyond measure.
It is our light, not our darkness that most frightens us.

We ask ourselves, Who am I to be brilliant,
gorgeous Talented, fabulous?
Actually, who are you not to be?
You are a child of God.

Your playing small, Doesn't serve the world.
There's nothing enlightened about shrinking
So that other people won't feel insecure around you.

We are meant to shine, as children do.
We were born to make manifest
The glory of God that is within us.
It's not just in some of us; It's in everyone

And as we let our own light shine.
We unconsciously give other people permission
To do the same.
As we're liberated from our own fear, Our presence
Automatically liberates others.

Fear is "an unpleasant emotion caused by the threat of danger, pain, or harm."[40] The question in the poem inspired me to think in the direction away from our personal fears towards examining the ability Jesus has given us to cause fear in the devil. What are you capable of doing in Christ that when you wake up

---
[39] Marianne Williams, *A Return to Love*, 1 Harper Collins, New York, 1992.
[40] www.lexico.com, 2022

in the morning, that may cause the enemy to have to dial 911 for back up? This is a question we might want to ask ourselves from time to time. Doing so, allows us to embrace the realization that there must be some value within us that threatens the enemy's peace, and causes us to experience the opposition we receive from the enemy through others. The scriptures teach us that the enemy of our soul is a thief, and he comes to steal, kill, and destroy (see John 10:10a). Thieves only come after that which is valuable. He wants your joy, your peace, your prosperity, etc. If you are only seeing the devil, and not what God is able to do through you, you are giving him free advertisement. Know that the emotional challenges you may be facing are because you are valuable and pose a threat to him.

> *What are you capable of doing in Christ that when you wake up in the morning, that may cause the enemy to have to dial 911 for back up?*

One of the greatest weapons we can use to combat the enemy, as stated previously, is to give him exactly what he doesn't want; that is for us not to succumb to his divisive schemes! Let's look at some of the ways the scriptures tell us we can give him exactly what he doesn't want through what Jesus taught in the beatitudes. The "be-attitudes" are what our attitude should be. Attitude is defined as, "a feeling or way of thinking that affects a person's behavior."[41]

> "Blessed are you who hunger now, For you shall be filled. Blessed are you who weep now, For you shall laugh, Blessed are you when men hate you, And when they exclude you, And revile you, and cast

---

[41] https://www.merriam-webster.com

out your name as evil, For the Son of Man's sake.
Rejoice in that day and leap for joy! For indeed your
reward is great in heaven,
For in like manner their fathers did to the prophets."
Luke 6:21-23

Jesus further taught the multitude about what their attitude should be towards their enemies:

"But I say to you, love your enemies, bless those
who curse you, do good to those who hate you, and
pray for those who spitefully use you and persecute
you, that you may be sons of your Father in heaven;
for He makes His sun to rise on the evil and on the
good, and sends rain on the just and the unjust."
Matthew 5:44-45

By applying the teachings of Jesus in our lives, we will give the enemy a response according to the Word of God, rather than a knee jerk reaction with our emotions. The right attitude in response to our challenging situations will determine our altitude because it will cause us to rise above our emotions and see things from a heavenly perspective.

Another definition for attitude is, "a position assumed for a specific purpose."[42] Having a heavenly perspective about your situation shifts your position and creates a distance, like being thousands of miles high in an airplane. Posturing yourself above your situation will cause things to appear smaller, having less of an emotional effect upon us. Satan was evicted from heaven and sent to the earth, (see Luke 10:18, Ezekiel

---

[42] https://www.merriam-webster.com

28:16). He attempts to pull us emotionally, like gravity, which represents our flesh, to hinder us from executing a heavenly attitude towards our challenges. There is earth's view of your situation and then there is heaven's view.

By applying the teachings of Jesus in our lives, we will give the enemy a response according to the Word of God, rather than a knee jerk reaction with our emotions.

> "And He raised us up together with Him and made us sit down together [giving us joint seating with Him] in the heavenly sphere [by virtue of our being] in Christ Jesus (the Messiah, the Anointed One)."
> Ephesians 2:6, AMPC

Giving the enemy what he doesn't want occurs when we accept and walk in who God has created us to be and allow ourselves to be used to touch the lives of others.

> "Heal the sick, cleanse the lepers, raise the dead, cast out demons. Freely you have received, freely give."
> Matthew 10:8

> "For we are God's [own] handiwork (His workmanship), recreated in Christ Jesus, [born anew] that we may do those good works which God predestined (planned beforehand) for us [taking paths which He prepared ahead of time], that we would walk in them [living the good life which He prearranged and made ready for us to live]."
> Ephesians 2:10, AMPC

"And [so that you can know and understand]
what is the immeasurable and unlimited and
surpassing greatness of His power in and for us who
believe, as demonstrated in the working of
His mighty strength."
Ephesians 1:19, AMPC

Selah Moment: Holy Spirit spoke to me one day about using me to communicate the love of the Father to others. I said, "How can I be used in this area when I have felt so unloved myself at times." He said, 'Who best would be able to minister to their need to feel loved, but someone that knows what it feels like and knows what is needed to receive healing.'" Yes, as God's children, we have meat inside of us to do His will and that can be a threat to the enemy! The areas we find ourselves challenged in can be the very area that God wants to use us in.

List below some of your past and current challenges and allow Holy Spirit to show you how God can use it for His glory, your good, and for the healing of others.

_____

_____

_____

_____

_____

_____

_____

_____

Is There Any Meat on the Bones?

_____

_____

_____

_____

_____

_____

_____

_____

_____

_____

_____

_____

_____

"He comforts us in all our troubles so that we can comfort others. When they are troubled, we will be able to give them the same comfort God has given us."
II Corinthians 1:4, NLT

Chapter 15
A Message to Leaders

Some leaders may experience situations regarding ministry that can cause them to only see the "bones" and not the "meat" of what God is doing. A leader's focus can become blinded by the challenges of ministry. It's always a challenge when we work with people and their various personalities—after all, people will be people! Your interaction is not just with the various personalities; you will also be dealing with the baggage of hurt they bring with them, sometimes from other congregations. If that baggage is not recognized and ministered to, you will have what my husband terms as a *Spiritually Transmitted Disease* (STD) to contend with. It's always wise to "wait and watch" before releasing an individual into a position within the congregation where they can potentially do any damage, to you or your congregation,

A leader's focus can become blinded by the challenges of ministry.

regardless of what their resume might say or how urgent the need is in your church.

It is very important that leaders, especially pastors, allow themselves to be human *beings* and not just human *doings*. Becoming a leader doesn't mean that you stop feeling. Leaders often get hurt and God doesn't want them to walk in denial of that fact. Acknowledge that hurt because knowing is half the battle. We can't fight what is hidden from us but once it comes into the light, we will have more of a fighting chance. Pastor Larry Fannin, a wise pastor from Indiana, once spoke something I thought was very profound in one of his sermons: "Every living organism must get rid of its waste, flush and go!" If we don't eliminate the hurts we encounter as leaders, it will cause us to get stuck. I have heard many leaders say they are experiencing "spiritual burnout" in regard to ministry. However, a spirit can't burn out. Our body and soul can because we haven't taken time to receive ministry for ourselves.

Becoming a leader doesn't mean that you stop feeling.

I was a part of the dance ministry while I was also pastoring one of Evangel's outreach churches in Detroit, Michigan. I had the opportunity to attend a dance conference in Columbus, Ohio. At one of the sessions, a famous speaker and author began to teach on Moses and the fact that he had experienced disappointment with the people he was leading. During that sermon, involuntary tears began to roll down my face. That word brought deliverance and revelation of the deep hurt and disappointment I felt towards others, myself, and God that I harbored unconsciously. After scheduling myself for a weekend shut-in with the Lord, I prayed and asked Holy Spirit to show me anyone that I needed to forgive, including God and myself. The list that He gave me yielded over seventy-five people! Being strong doesn't mean we don't acknowledge our woundedness; it takes more strength to ignore our hurts, because they build momentum, than it takes to acknowledge and allow God to heal them.

It takes more strength to ignore our hurts, because they build momentum, than it takes to acknowledge and allow God to heal them.

Sometimes being a leader can seem like a thankless job. We may feel taken for granted at times. There may be times when we don't so much as get a "goodbye" from members we have trusted, who have been with us for a while, and we had expected to continue with us. How many times have we received disappointing letters from people we have been with through sickness, disease, joy, and sorrow saying they are moving on or pointing out all of the things wrong with us or the ministry? Some leaders may have received phone calls in the middle of the night and responded to members in crisis, yet those same members couldn't take the time to pick up the phone or ask for a meeting to share their intentions to leave! It has always amazed me that people are unable to hear from God for anything else and request our assistance, but when they feel it's time to move on, they can hear so clearly from God leaving their leader out of the decision. These and similar experiences can cause woundedness that needs to be acknowledged and submitted for healing.

It will be very helpful to leaders if they can grasp that the message God gives is always to the messenger first. Continual growth will not take place in your own life if you only spend time with the Lord to get a message for others and not allow Him to speak to you about you. Your continual growth will ignite growth in your congregation. This can lessen the possibility

The message God gives is always to the messenger first. of frustration and aggravation within you because you are not witnessing the growth in your people you would like to see. It's always easy to teach what we know, but it's who we are that is reproduced in those under us. The congregation will reflect the leader because the leader's job is to reproduce themselves as Jesus reproduced Himself in His disciples.

Whenever I review my past sermons, I realize that many of them reflected the season I was in personally and alert me to the necessity of spending more time digesting the message for myself *first*, for any self-application needed. You will not be as effective if you become too excited about receiving a good message from the Lord to share with the congregation before you meditate on it and allow Holy Spirit to show you if you can also benefit from it. Some things you will be able to teach, but there are some things that will be gained through them observing you and how you apply God's Word to your own life.

I don't take pleasure in saying this, but I have ministered to many people who have been hurt by leaders using their position to violate them emotionally, mentally, financially, and even sexually. Damaged people will damage others. Leaders should *never* use the Word to manipulate, control or place people in bondage, so they can feel more in charge. Ask Holy Spirit if you might have issues of control because we control out of fear. Most leaders, understandably, want things to be right, especially if they see their works as a reflection of themselves. After all, one of the signs of good leadership is the ability to get things done. Therefore, it becomes very important that as leaders we don't use our position of influence for personal gain. Peter's advice to elders gives instructions on how leaders are to relate to their congregation:

"Shepherd the flock of God which is among
you, serving as overseers, not by compulsion but
willingly, not for dishonest gain but eagerly; nor as
being lords over those entrusted to you, but being
examples to the flock; and when the Chief Shepherd
appears, you will receive the crown of glory that
does not fade away."
I Peter 5:2-4, NLT

Here are some practical ideas that I have learned over the years that I believe may be useful in helping leaders separate the "meat from the bones," when it comes to interacting with and growing their congregation spiritually:

- Get in touch with your own vulnerability because what you don't know can hurt you. The enemy will send people to pull on you in the area that you are the weakest. If you deal with loneliness, he will send people to tempt you in that area to entice you to sin. Being a leader is not a prison term to keep you from having a life. Only you make it that way by not scheduling yourself in to have a life.

- Most leaders will represent a parent or close authority figure to some people in their congregation. Be conscious of and sensitive to your ability to cause potential hurt for those who are vulnerable to further hurt from those in authority. You are in a great position to bring

Being a leader is not a prison term to keep you from having a life. Only you make it that way by not scheduling yourself in to have a life.

healing to them in that area by allowing the agape love of the Father to flow through you to them. If you see yourself as their spiritual parent as stated previously, then the inclination to date your sons and daughters, (a type of spiritual incest and abuse of position), will not be an area of temptation. I have ministered to many people who have been victims of this type of abuse.

- Fellowshipping with your congregation shouldn't be your only socialization. God can send those of your same level of leadership or above that you can be divinely connected with to help you in this area. Being in covenant with those of your same leadership level or above, provide accountability. It will also provide you with a safe place to vent, get wisdom, and prayer for what you might be going through emotionally.

- It may appear at times that you are more appreciated by those outside of your home, but it is not the heart of God for home to be neglected for the purpose of ministry. Prioritizing your family will close the door to the enemy who will try and enter your back door by bringing rejection, anger, resentment, etc., to spouses and children because they feel less important than the ministry. Our first ministry starts at home. Traditionally, leaders are mostly trained for the functioning in the church building and not as much for the strengthening of their family.

- Our primary assignment as leaders is to lead people to Jesus and the principles of the Kingdom of God and not to ourselves. This will help eliminate false responsibilities, false burdens that can cause leadership to begin to feel inadequate and overwhelmed. Feeling overwhelmed may cause a leader in their frustration, to take their anger out on the congregation. The shepherd is to lead the sheep by still waters, (Psalms 23:2), not beat them with angry words. Taking on these false responsibilities or burdens can lead to legalism where we try to control things with too many rules and regulations, trying to avoid the possibility of future emotional suffering from negative outcomes.

- Acknowledge and deal with any insecurities or social anxiety you may wrestle with. This will present a hesitation when it comes to confronting things that need to be addressed to bring proper alignment to individuals or to the congregation. The fear of rejection and /or being judged will lead one to avoidance which will later end up in frustration because you will be working against yourself. It helped me tremendously when Bishop Jerry taught leadership that confrontation should be seen as a positive move, done in love, for the purpose of building up the person.

God has called leaders to be an instrument of healing, but we can only do that when we are able to see past the flaws in others and see their needs. When leaders are hurt themselves, their ability to help others heal will be hindered. The following is one of my favorite poems that helped to refocus my role in ministry many days:

"The Prayer of St. Francis of Assisi"[43]

Lord, make me an instrument of your peace
Where there is hatred, let me bring love.
Where there is offence, let me bring pardon,
Where there is discord, let me bring union
Where there is error, let me bring truth.
Where there is doubt, let me bring faith.
Where there is despair, let me bring hope
Where there is darkness, let me bring Your light.
Where there is sadness, let me bring joy.
O Master, let me not seek as much
to be consoled as to console,
to be understood as to understand,
to be loved as to love,
for it is in giving that one receives,
it is in self-forgetting that one finds,
it is pardoning that one is pardoned,
it is in dying that one is raised to eternal life.

---

[43] Francis, Giuliano Ferri, & Sala, E. *The Prayer of St. Francis* (2013)

Selah Moment: God has graced us leaders for the race. He has not called us as leaders because we were so qualified. He called us so He could qualify us. *"And God is able to make all grace abound towards you, that you, always having all sufficiency in all things, may have an abundance for every good work" (II Corinthians 9:8).*

List below any vulnerable areas you see in your life as a leader, submit to Holy Spirit to receive God's empowering grace.

_____

_____

_____

_____

_____

_____

_____

"That you may walk worthy of the Lord, fully
pleasing Him, being fruitful in every good work
and increasing in the knowledge of God; strengthened with
all might, according to His glorious power,
for all patience and longsuffering with joy."
Colossians 1:10-11

Epilogue

(A Second Look)

I began this book using the example of the Apostle Paul written in *chapter three of the book of Philippians, verse 12: "Not that I have already attained, either were already perfect: but I follow after, if that I may apprehend that for which also I am apprehended of Christ Jesus."* He shared his goal but he also gave his strategy for accomplishing that goal:

> "No, dear brothers and sisters, I have not achieved it, but I focus on this one thing: Forgetting the past and looking forward to what lies ahead, I press on to reach the end of the race and receive the heavenly prize for which God, through Christ Jesus, is calling us."
> Verses 13-14, NLT

This book has been mainly about focus and being able to see beyond the hurts of life and seeing Jesus, getting His view of our circumstances through the use of scripture. Applying God's Word, along with examples found in Scripture showing others in similar circumstances, will provide emotional healing as you see God's meat and press on.

> "Now all these things happened to them as examples, and they were written for our admonition, upon whom the ends of the ages have come."
> I Corinthians 10:11.

The Apostle Paul had many things in his past that could be used to hold him back, but he chose to not let it be his focus. Instead, he chose to look ahead, much like Christ did when He died on the cross for us.

> "Looking away [from all that will distract] to Jesus, Who is the Leader and the Source of our faith [giving the first incentive for our belief] and is also its Finisher [bringing it to maturity and perfection]. He, for the joy [of obtaining the prize] that was set before Him, endured the cross, despising and ignoring the shame, and is now seated at the right hand of the throne of God."
> Hebrews 12:2, AMPC

Throughout this book, I have shared parts of my story which I consider His-story of loving kindness, faithfulness, and healing. My continued praise and testimony is found in *II Samuel 22:20, NLT: "He brought me forth into a large place; He delivered me because He delighted in me."*

This is how I felt when He sent me to Evangel Christian Churches in Roseville, Michigan. He placed me in a large place so I could heal and grow. I haven't been connected with them for over thirty-two years because it is a perfect church with perfect leaders and perfect people. I wasn't there by God to zero in on their imperfections. God placed me there because His anointing for healing, restoration, and equipping was there for me. There is no perfect church as they are all filled with imperfect people. Many may come to church expecting to have a cruise ship experience. God's true church is a battleship, training our hands to war and our fingers to fight the assignments of the enemy on our lives, our family, and others, and to bring as many souls into the Kingdom of God as we can!

> "Praise the Lord who is my rock.
> He trains my hands for war and my fingers skill
> for battle."
> Psalms 144:1, NLT

In our modern day, the availability of media platforms to bring church into our homes has been a blessing to many who are physically unable to attend regular church services. However, it can also be used as a means for some who have been hurt by their experience in church to avoid the possibility of future hurt.

There is a corporate anointing we can tap into when we attend a house of worship that you will not experience being at home. Red Rover is one of the games we frequently played as children, during which two teams lined up facing each other. A player rushes the opposition's line in an effort to break through their joined hands. The interlocking of the individual hands forms a stronghold against the challenger. The same thing applies in the spirit. There is a strength obtained when we operate in numbers, in the church and in the Body of Christ.

> "Two people are better off than one, for they can help each other succeed."
> Ecclesiastes 4:9, NLT

I would also like to take this opportunity to briefly address those who have decided that the organized church is not relevant because of its shortcomings. I am reminded that Jesus, who is our example and not man, addressed the negative things that were happening in the synagogue, especially in the religious leaders, yet He still attended, taught, and participated in the feasts. He didn't tell them to tear down the building and freelance, but He was used as an agent of change who reminded them what the true purpose of His Father's house was; a house of prayer (Matt. 21:13; Mark 11:17; Luke 19:46). It's very easy to stand on the sidelines and point out the problem but God has called us to be a part of the solution.

Maybe you were raised in church, a child of a leader or, like me, came into church as an adult with preconceived notions of church people and experienced disappointment and hurt on many occasions. Prayerfully, this book will assist you in allowing God to heal your hurt, and change your view concerning organized church, so you can be used by him to be a true representative of His church.

> "Let us hold tightly without wavering to the hope we affirm, for God can be trusted to keep His promise. Let us think of ways to motivate one another to acts of love and good works. And let us not neglect our meeting together, as some people do, but encourage one another, especially now that the day of His return is drawing near."
> Hebrews 10:23-25, NLT

I pray this book has been helpful to the reader bringing thoughtful consideration to some of the painful things you have encountered in your Christian walk which may have detoured you along the way. God is always wanting to strengthen His house and our individual houses from the inside out. Let it begin this day forward in you. Allow the fires of revival to be kindled in you as you continue on the path God has chosen for you. Allow His healing power to sharpen your focus to look for the possibility of meat on the bones you may encounter while you are doing life.

> "The Lord bless you and keep you; the Lord make His face shine upon you, and be gracious to you; the Lord lift up His countenance upon you, and give you peace."
> Numbers 6:24-26

Suggested Reading List

You Can Be Emotionally Free, Rita Bennet, Bridge-Logos, Gainesville, Florida, 1982, 2001, 2005

Making Peace With Your Past, Dr. H. Norman Wright, Revell, Grand Rapids, Michigan, 1985, 2013

Inner Healing Through Healing of Memories, Betty Tapscott, Betty Tapscott Publishing, 1975

Love Like You've Never Been Hurt, Jentezen Franklin, Chosen Books, Bloomington Minnesota, 2018

Spiritual Warfare: A Comprehensive Guide To Personal Healing and Deliverance, Drs. Jerry & Sherill Piscopo with Simon & Trish Presland, Xulon Press, Maitland, Florida, 2013

Healing The Wounded Heart, Removing obstacles to Intimacy with God, Thom Gardner, Destiny Image Publishers, Shippensburg, Pennsylvania, 2005

A Tale of Three Kings: A Study In Brokenness, Gene Edwards, Tyndale Publishers, Carol Stream, Illinois, 1980, 1992

Total Forgiveness, R. T. Kendall, Charisma House, Lake Mary, Florida, 2002, 2007

Forgiving our Parents Forgiving Ourselves, Dr. David Stoop, Revell, Grand Rapids, 1991, 1996, 2011

Forgiving What You'll Never Forget, Dr. David Stoop, Revell, Grand Rapids, 2001, 2003

When Your Bad Meets His Good: Finding Purpose In Your Pain, Kimberly Jones-Pothier, Charisma House, Lake Mary, Florida, 2013

Boundaries: When to Say Yes, How to Say No to Take Control of Your Life, Dr. Henry Cloud & Dr. John Townsend, Zondervan, Grand Rapids, Michigan, 1992, 2017

Love Hunger, Drs. Minirth, Meier, Hemfelt, Sneed & Hawkins, Nashville, Tennessee, Thomas Nelson, 1990, 2004

Destroying the Spirit of Rejection, Apostle John Eckhardt, Charisma House, Lake Mary Florida, 2016

Search For Significance (Combined book & workbook), Robert S. McGee, Thomas Nelson, Nashville, Tennessee, 1998, 2003

About the Author

Dr. Sandra Gay co-labors with her husband, Dr. Alonzo T. Gay, Sr., as overseers of Acts Ministries Inc. of Eagle Lake, Florida. Dr. Sandra has a Master's Degree in Pastoral Counseling and a Doctor of Divinity. She was ordained as an Elder thirty years ago, and was recognized and installed through a presbytery in 2016 into the five-fold office of a Teacher. She previously directed and facilitated the Spiritual Warfare Seminars of Evangel Christian Churches of Roseville, Michigan for more than fourteen years. Dr. Sandra served as an Evangel Outreach Pastor in the inner city of Detroit for several years, and has been a faculty member of Destiny School of Ministry since its inception in 1998. She has traveled extensively, nationally and internationally, bringing forth impartation, revelation, and activation to the Body of Christ. She has a passion for prayer, worship, and the presence of the Lord.

Dr. Sandra uses her teaching and training skills and experience to develop team ministries, leaders, and to establish Inner Healing and Deliverance ministries in various churches and ministries. Isaiah 61:1-3 rings in her heart, as she brings a message of healing, deliverance, and restoration to the people of God.

To contact Dr. Sandra Gay:

Email:
authorsgay@gmail.com

Mailing Address:
P O Box 885
Eagle Lake, FL 33839

www.ingramcontent.com/pod-product-compliance
Lightning Source LLC
Chambersburg PA
CBHW042112120526
44592CB00042B/2700